RESPECT FOR LIFE

Ridding Humankind Of Shame

RUSSELINE J. KYLE

authorHOUSE®

AuthorHouse™
1663 Liberty Drive
Bloomington, IN 47403
www.authorhouse.com
Phone: 1 (800) 839-8640

Published by AuthorHouse   10/06/2015

ISBN: 978-1-5049-5363-4 (sc)
ISBN: 978-1-5049-5362-7 (e)

Print information available on the last page.

This book is printed on acid-free paper.

CONTENTS

"The material was the richest cloth of gold, which was found."
The words of Edgar Allan Poe

First let me say, I believe there will be persons who may express their dislike or likes for what I have written in regards to the human- race being slow in their unity with each other and other life forms on earth, and other contents spoken in my book. You may say to one-self; "do I really want to read this book"?

I would like people to read my book, my purpose is to bring light to some situations, and issues many are not thinking about, and those who need their consciousness to change for the best for all forms of life on the Planet to live in harmony and peace with each other in showing love and respect because all life should be respected. I want all of my fellow humans to realize and understand I know we all are wonderful creations from the Source of Life. Knowing it's just a blessing to be thought of in this plan of life. Just take a moment to think about it, for this moment you are blessed to be thought of to be created and a wonderful being as yourself. My desire is to assist humanity with my words not to criticize, hoping the true reality will overcome the blinding trickery's who are many, to be expose and to stop their misuse, and their ability to control others, causing sorrow and pain. Sorry too say, there are those who allowed their minds to be in salved willingly. Many overlooking their own inner strength and their ability to sense what is right or in error and attract information from the True Source of life from within oneself to make the plan of life work for all of life.

Since some may think I am to forward in my Forewords and Introduction, wait until you get into the book. Believe it or not this book is about wake-up call in regards to the realization of societies and ones own true-self.

When you become willing to open your mind to the richness of the realties in life then this book will be for you to read, just think about it, maybe it will open many of your minds to things not thought about in the past? And then you say Okay, maybe this book is for me to read.

I would like to say this "All Life Is ONE" All life-forms are our brothers and sisters in creation, the only different, is the higher and the lower in evolvement. Should I say, all of creation is one, and we should Love with a Divine Love for all life. I need to clarify my statement; I myself see people as consciousness or mind, living in a body with ability to think: knowledge is what determines the power of ones growth or evolvement, we humans must become conscious of the unlimited world within and around us, I know we humans as being's "consciousness" are some time in an illusion - world and many moved oneself away from reality placing one-self in the mind frame that we as humans are greater then or more importance then other forms of Life." Not So" This thought has held us humans away from other forms of life with the idea that we are more evolved, in reality, not so know, we humans are only one part of this, so-call plan of life. In reading the book you will not be disappointed, this book I hope will change your life for the better, in exploring life and all its beauty. SO IT IS, IT'S DONE

This book is written in love offered to you as a wake-up tool, for your inner true knowing, it only points in the direction where you can find answers for yourself. As you read this book, images the necessary clues as to what is right action on your part. In doing so, you have a new sense of confidence and courage in love for yourself and your own judgment. Although you personally have no specific issue in mine at this time a single question, a simple prayer will suffice.

My intention, of writing this book is only to assist and empower you as an individual in service to life on earth and life in general.

FOREWORD

This book is written because of the need for change in humanity consciousness, knowing those of us who are concern for the survival of life on this planet will change, for the better knowing it needs to be.

The factors of theology and the sciences are somewhat dogmatic in their views about life, leaving no space for acceptance of new views or techniques for change in the survival for our betterment, only for the so-call, after- life or nothingness. The theologian sees the Source of life as one who places us in hell or heaven. Many of the scientific concept declares there's no God and or every Aton, stands awed before their unfolding Comic drama, leaving space for us humans to arrange the plan of life to our own liking.

Both of these groups need to combine their efforts in getting a true concept in what's life; knowing there is a higher knowing to be had beyond ones natural eyes to see, knowing life is perfection in its making through the original plan by our Maker.

The real purpose is for all to unfold to the oneness of one's true relative nature as being individual entities evolving into ones owned Spiritual-Conscious- Nature and Being, which directs ones lower-self to the higher-self becoming a being of mastery of one's own mind and soul being filled with Spirit control, to be progressive as ones true-self or god-person whichever it may be in image required.

The philosophy of life sprung forth through various experiences and the measure in which people prepare for navigation of one's present life. As humans, by merely learning naturally opens the channels of one's mind primarily to unify mind with a form of faith (confidence) in which one will achieve awareness and perception to be successful in their lives.

Hopefully, each individual will with a noble intellectual conscience attempt to penetrate the structure and relations of one's environment, and unproductive eliminate those activities, habits and, issues which cause resulting in the need for individual lessons to assume a sufficient reality will change for the betterment of ones life.

In each individual, there is an ever circling of birth, death and rebirth, which manifest moment to moment, and we are being governed by the law of Life's energy, one increase in one's awareness and perception, all aspect of learning will reveal itself, just as the concept of physical rebirth is used for the evolvement of humankind Mind or Soul-Consciousness. This reality needs to be achieved, as soon as one comes into the realization that humankind is not just flesh and bone, as one open to that reality one will expand in consciousness overcoming the barrier of ignorance which blocks one from becoming one's true-self. Don't let anyone make you feel lesser than you are; A divine creature of wonder, you are wonderfully created, whatever your physical make-up it mean nothing, the outer form is only ones body (veil) which one works though, ones inside what's matters, the true-person, the real you. There are peoples who would try too be-litter you, don't let them do it, the only flaw is in ones own consciousness by choice.

Many of mankind is enchanted through their minds to find the answer to pleasure of the physical, (mental and emotional desire), not what's true reality. Most people permit their emotions and egotisms to run wild, using their lower instinctive facility to be uncontrollable. They have no real clue, of what real life can bring.

In servicing ones lower nature only causes the individual to be slow one in finding the true realities, which comes as one realize it takes seeking truth and discrimination in all ones activities in order for expansion of one's consciousness to meet the requirement for one's higher consciousness to unfold to it's highest level.

Truth about different activities will be given to direct those who sincerely desire one's life crest to be victorious, harmonious and knowing it will also promote clarity, which sooths the repressed and depressed individuals. There are, no doubt a new existence many are seeking, will come, it is necessary to look more closely into the problems, which determines the connection of nature and the limit of problems in life.

We are consciousness, many produce ideas in ignorance not using caution in what will be the outcome of the action, which causes one to need correction or one knowingly produce that which is not constructive for the best in one's life, one can look for the attraction or magnetisms of whatever, one send into the universe, where it's ones intention or not it will effect ones true-self, and if one works in the so-call evilness it will work in one's own life. There are acceptances to this rule, now that's another story, which would not be given in this book. All attentions are about life in general as we know life to be, other things would pull the book away from my original intent, only open the door to the knowledge many are not awaken to, or willing to accept at this time. This is another project forth coming for others who are willingness to awake to whether to create good or bring light on evil manifestations.

The most important thing now is to be a self-conscious being, knowing whatever thoughts are created in ones own - mind and coupled with ones outer emotional desire attracts in physical form, which causes the manifestation.

The power, within you, is the same "Power" which permits all life forms to exist and function in the blindness of their present consciousness it's dormant until one starts to work toward evolvement in their own individual self-expression.

Our aspirations of existence need to be examined more directly on an individual bases to obtain change. A better life on this planet can be achieved not only for mankind but for all life here. In reality there is nothing created without being a form of life?

We know indirectly by our minds and bodily senses all existence, is real even those unlike us as humans in form other creatures; are forms of the same creative nature of life, each go's in its own way separate beings and yet they are the same in nature even the plants and the elements want their own existence to be untouched by others who do not even understand their own likes or differences and ones similarity.

Life defines its own treasures although it does not separate vast need for all forms of life to expand in the plan of evolution of existence in the same way, but all are pushing toward becoming in the Realm of just being at this time.

In the oneness of life, every form of life or stage of life is an awakening to the need for the benefits from which the various differences in the qualities of things, we all need. It can be easily explained if one is willing to open one's mind, think about it, what are some of these things we all share? Question, is it the biological or simply a chance for mental immortality of our being or is it the simple things like water, food, air, light, and darkness, not just the extended serve of mind, body and spirit as one's own self for the use of one's emotional life in faith, love, and fear.

These are things on this planet all of us share in expression.

We all are creatures of our own physical vehicles which manifest our own existence and we share the same elements and receive the same benefits as one. All breathe the air, drink the water, and eat the fruits from Mother-Earth, and we all get exactly the same results satisfaction of one's need for survival, and to live to express one's own purpose in life.

Likewise, all qualities of the elements and what represents the life existence is in emotions, thoughts, and feelings, of love, hate, etc., were felt by each living thing and there is a constant flow of energy to distribute these qualities. As one entertain their chosen stream of life, the nature of that form spreads their influence to flourish and empower others or to devalue others by dishonesty and destructive activity.

Respect life, knowing life is ageless and endless in sacred and holds all captive and has all capabilities for the Relative life on Earth.

We are to eliminate the wide ranges of ignorance and be expanded into the reality of truth by letting all of your matter senses to integrate and find truth, using the brain most of all to remove old bad habits, that has settled in the sub-conscious-mind, it's time to let the left side of one's brain integrates fully with the right by removing the bad programs in the sub-conscious part of the brain so it can become one explosive power source that will permit the opening of one's mind to the mysteries of the Universe and one's higher-self.

Remember, all of creations on this planet have the same need to evolve their lives. All life shares these needs together. We all feel love, and desire, although many of us use that which opposes the good, like hatred, greed and the cravings, for only the physical gratifications of one's being.

We shape our own destiny for success by evolving to the place in consciousness of god- consciousness and perfection, if desired. When you begin to try to experience the conviction of these words 'we shape our own destiny" another world will open to you, and you will move on into the new way of thinking about yourself and no longer living in the false sense of who and what you are. You are all creative entities of the gods just as everything else on the planet, so pursue truth, and respect life.

When you read this book try to read at-times, when you feel peaceful, say to yourself "I close the door to all distractions and gaze on the inner meaning of these words."

In writing this book, I felt the need to address some issues all of humanity must face now or in the future. This book is to plant a seed of love in the hearts of my fellow humans.

Life is full of challenges and oppositions to resolve, as we face these blocks in our pathway to our life success and fulfillment, we are expected to meet the challenges with confidence to take control.

I do not expect every reader will immediately understand the gravity of the message being brought or the situation that we are facing, yet something keeps you wondering why? There are those who do not want people to be informed of the different barriers in place. It's time to wake up accept what has presented within this book, and it's so much more I cannot speak about, if you desire to be somewhat free in mind, read my book. I therefore include some elements that common to all levels of awareness to the average person, hopefully it will assist you in the start of a new reality.

Discovering the magic of life is the challenge joining us in connecting back to the original state of unity with all forms on planet earth. This is the ideal state which allows one to express ones existence directly by non-conceptually or without judgment, in approaching life, letting things be as they are unconditioned reflecting as a mirror is willing to reflect anything from all levels

Once you start exploring life in its fullness, the beauty will come, and darkness will be hard to accept in the future. Some will seek truth and some will not, there are those who will seek happiness and will not find it, others are weak, to their emotional side and they will suffer, through their desires from others, which will be non-coming, they will be disappointed from whom they seek;

Positive growth only comes through change within your-self first however one may involve a descent into darkness as a part of the cycle of perpetual evolvement. One must be awaken to the knowledge that all of nature in its progression consists of the six aspects in life; birth, decay, death, fertilization, gestation, and rebirth.

There are many questions that come to one's mind in trying to understand life and the purpose for being? What's my Purpose and true nature? Why was I Born? What will my Challenges be? And what is my Destiny?

When one asked these questions of oneself, you may think long and hard about your life experiences and the possibilities for your new birth, your true nature, and nature is a constellation of possibilities and a surrounded and circumscribed by different impossibilities.

By examining ones limitations: your limitations is supported by your reality of what you believe life to be, it becomes clearer to you, you will begin to see various notions your hopes about yourself which are not supported by the real activity working in your life at present, but one can change the events to process a new future.

Questioning yourself; "Why was I Born," you may be thinking, "I must have come into the world for the satisfaction and the will of a higher power to be empower to continue growth and to keep my will in the will of Divine Will."

What will ones challenges, the question of the conditions one life is lived in present and maybe or of the past. And it the question of your pattern of adversity, one must undergo in order to increase in self-awareness and self-truth, to question is the answer.

As for ones Destiny means your ideals are passage through life with you, ideals with future possibilities of improvement. It also means the Divine desire for your Highest Good, knowing there is no bad destiny for you as you grow toward your Divine Source of Life. Your Destiny is your Spiritual Destination.

Letting go of all the centuries parenting which have brought pain and sorrow to the life forms on earth, let go the past and encompass all life that dwells within the earth, in order to intensified your growth, which let you see with a loving heart and you will learn to be respectful to all life, knowing we must life in accordance with the will of our Divine Source of Creation.

First you must trust in yourself, than you can trust in the earth and all states of being in the progress of evolvement of your true-self.

"Live life to its fullness, so it shall be"

INTRODUCTION

There are events, which has caused slow achievements for humankind in the areas of self-evolvement or what we call Spiritual- Consciousness, or Christ-Consciousness. All is self- improved through the Source of life. We know that mankind is swayed by the devices and moods of the moment and many are slaves to their own craving.

Every action has for itself an end reaction, by mirroring itself and dominates one's aim which is its nature, it must complete in itself.

I am not here to tell you there is nothing wrong or matters, as you believe in the Source of all life, and live your individuality as a good person, or when you are kept in the blind on issues whether effects you personally or not, and you feel or believe it doesn't matter, you are living in an imaginative world, what effect one effects another, we all are made from the same substance (energy) of life. Many believe that saying," out of sight, out of mind," have no fears all will be okay and keeping on about one's personal business, not assuring change.

There is no escaping the past activities or the present conditions that humans have developed. At present all that can be done is for one to be mindful of ones own activities and investigate all situations, and try to govern your own life for improvement.

You may question what are the situations that govern one's life?

'Knowing one of the most important things is for a person to be open to learning.

All humanity have the ability to learn beyond other creatures as we have been told and it's been taught, the lower animals are born only with sensation and memory, I wonder, is this statement true? Think about it do we really know or study to be true?

Yes, there are some more intelligent and capable of learning than those who do not have the gift of memory as many think. Although those who cannot remember, the ones who cannot hear sounds, for instance Bees and others of similar creatures as we been told are without the ability to learn are said to be slower in their achievement as the ones with hearing and memories. Most Animal do live by impressions and memories, they have little in the way of connected experience, as it been said, just because we cannot understand their language, think about it, someone comes up to you speaking a language unknown to you there is no communication. Whereas, the human being has the ability to sense through their five senses along with the ability of memory and reasoning of mind to learn, we don't really know about the other life-forms totally. One overlooked the vibration state involves by all creative ethics in its state.

Because of mankind ability over the other creature's as it has been said, although our belief is to or one aim is to be productive in doing better in how we live in the practical sense. As, one becomes open to the knowledge of the relative principles and causes, then one will be free to act accordingly, they will be free to grow to increasingly produce competitive values for others and ones society and will have captured the purpose of life.

We as humans cannot use that saying; "A man of experience know that a thing is so, but do not really know why it is so." Mankind knows the reasons how and why of their handy-work in life, now one may not want to face it. One cannot use that old excuse to justify ones actions.

Humankind frame their own destiny, understand if a person is confuse and set in their own comfort zone of one's ignorance's, do not pursue knowledge in order to understand, she/he is powerless in developing one's own life, they are destined to failure, until their mind become open to truth, than can one move forward in overcoming life's challenges.

The purpose of this writing is to raise the conscious of those who act wrongly to change their present activities, which are undesirable to become a constructive developer of societies for the well being of all life on this planet earth.

We all have lived in a world of crisis, from the very began of so-call time there has been no peace among the people of earth, for centenaries we have been going in circles and the need for elaboration on the causes which has brought us to the place where change is necessary, the events of the past and present has cause us to face the issues to this point in history, it's essential. Mankind nature is to question and know the reasons for their difficult in life.

The greatest minds in history have seen the signs, guess you are wondering why things hasn't change?

Mankind has forsaken the law of life and has change the course of the river of life; the wise ones have tried to change the minds and hearts of mankind for centuries, but hardening of mankind heart kept growing, even in the effort of the wise ones, the majority refuses to learn from their mistakes, it's a hard pull to get one to face or accept their mistakes and to be willing to see truth about oneself.

The mighty directing intelligence has clothe each of us in itself and carry us to whatever direction we desire for ourselves, forward or backward. Our freedom gives us the power to choose and the choice is our making. If one chose disappointments you remember it's your fault, not because you had committed any wrong, it's because your mind has embraced failure by ones doubts and sometime poor judgment or perhaps listening to wrong suggestions there are many reasons, one must analyze oneself to see in what decision could have been the cause of it all.

By understanding the different degrees of our existence, being the first principles of reality, many appear to be lost to the cure. In confronting the causes, one must understand, first what mankind true makeup is?

The average human mind is clouded with superficial concerns and creations. There are those who feel, that we are thrown into this world with no choice in the matter the only certainty; we are born and we will die out of the body. We come into the world naked and clueless of what is required of us. Preoccupied with appearances and disconnection from our real self, caring many to turn into a selective groups, the worst and most hopeless aspects of human existence; many become acutely aware of darkest, ugliness and the most evil aspects of mankind existence, and there are those who are just the opposite.

To bring people to the consciousness of what is right, and that is to respect life and rid humanity of shame, it's not in the form of condemning or being judgmental, but out of love for humanity, and to enlighten and assist others in their recognition of their incorrect activities and learn from it to improve in the present and make way for a brighter future in their activities living by the laws layout for us, the law of Goodness.

In order for humanity to evolve in consciousness, we must make corrections in judgment by the experiences of one's past so we can stop being haunted by unworthy efforts in the form of non- constructive activities.

There are those who feel caged, caught in a nightmarish world, and their field of vision is dark and ominous, the general atmosphere is unbearable, they feel tortured physically and mentally, why continue in this way?

Without understanding of the why and how and without a clear solution for the problems that face them, and without a sense of purpose in life it can only be plainness or blankness. The wise ones know that a guide line is in order and that the reason for life is to be a noble product of creation, we must learn to see truth, if we haven't learned this truth the human race is doomed in their evolutional growth in consciousness.

Without a commitment to the survival of humankind, civilization as we desire will cease to unfold and become only a dream.

We seem to be turning back to the primitive way of thinking; get you before you get me, this is not the way civilization services life only destroys. Deception is on the rise in all areas; this has allowed an increase in specialization in the human character, which has caused many to suffer at the hands of those who enforce deceit.

We are gaining progress in technology, medicine and the sciences, question where dose the morality and nobility of the human spirit fit in?

There must be a deprogramming of persons who feel being deceptive is the only way, this must stop. All non-constructive activity of these persons must reverse, to allow the enfoldment of their higher consciousness, which leads to ones divine nature. We understand that civilization have sort many ways in search of the perfect dream, even to the point of wiping their opponents out of existence to get their so-call dream.

Instant of doing the noble things many are taking the opportunity to support their own desires for whatever it may be right or wrong to obtain it. When mistakes are made and accepted, the thought of being wrong is rejected in so many; ones restitution is out of the question.

Man exist and nature exist and one seek to know how and the reasons why the events are happening in their personal world and dropping over into the universe around them?

The generation of energy vibrations coming from each of us has an effect on the whole Universe. Whatever steps we take whether positive or non-constructive accelerates a creative effort in the surrounding atmosphere cause alteration of the natural order of things.

All too often many are educated in the IQ level of general reasoning or religious Systems, viewpoints without a clue of the real meaning or insight in the effects of all connections.

Let's simplify, first in classifying mankind in the Christianity argument by Paul; stated, humans are beings made-up of three parts, body, soul, and spirit, this definition is accepted by Christian theology as Paul's threefold division, but it tell us little about the different in the three, or mainly the soul and spirit. In reality mankind is a sevenfold entity or seven principles condensed into the three major division's spirit, soul and body.

Spirit, ones immortal self or divine Monad, the spiritual first veil of Atman, means self every being no matter how small or how great is a self, all of these selves derived from the Cosmic Life. Because the Atman nature is far above this human plane, so the first vehicle which it clothes itself was Buddha, this word mean to" awaken", so the Buddha faculty in humans lead to understanding because it awakes one into seeing things that one has been unaware. Many have interest in the general life of physical forms or matter, not concerned with world conditions as a whole.

Soul, there are two levels of one's soul one is the higher part of mind in when usual both sides of one's brain the right and left that is illuminated by the Buddha, or cosmic inspiration which is in the incarnated of the divine mind. The other is the lower part the ordinary left side brain-mind function ones human ego that drives energy, which is focused on desire.

Body the vital life's principles of energy, and the model framework of the physical body. We only see the visible matter, and we know all things are moved and motivated by invisible energies in their urges. There is a direct relationship between the invisible sixth-seventh human principles and the invisibility of nature.

The astral body is formed before birth, and its character is determined by causes created by ones ego in previous incarnations, that's another subject. It is called the Astral body or the model body, without the backing and cohesive semi-permanent astral model the body could not maintain its shape. After death of the physical body the astral constituents gradually resolve into their elements, while the emotional-mental principles remain semi-conscious until the final separation called the second death, that another story. In either case the physical aspect is the lowest of them all. Let go to the average simplest minds.

Many are trying to change the course in their lives we all know we need assistance from time to time to reach our goals. Even when one has obstructions and inadequacies knowing assistance from others one can achieve their goals. There are others who have needs; a person that is reaching but unable to touch the lifeline and no one is trying to place a line in their reach these are the ones who are destined to fail, if these persons have no one to assist them, We must realize it's our responsibility to assist them, but not to the lost of ones own survival. Many are in need and depend on others strength to assist them in removal the desolation that's taking place in their lives.

There are those who speak of change for the better, not understanding their heart and mind must come in agreement, they speak one thing and mean another, they are not putting forth the needed effort to achieve, and they mostly place the blame on things outside themselves.

In the human ignorance, mankind has position himself in only harm way, and the outside world is the blame, and it's out of the question to blame oneself for some of the mishaps, always looking for someone else to blame.

Yes, many of us are receiving the benefits of others labor whether right or wrong activity it brings the results and many enjoy, we accept the goods, but unwilling to take responsibility for one's own possibilities of non-productivity without effort.

Even though the average human lives in their own personal world and one's own abilities, which is limited to the development of one's personality and mental achievements, skills and until the aspiration of that person awakes to the understanding of life and its true purpose and sufficient spiritual undertaken it means little or nothing.

Until one is willing to take full charge of one's own life and see oneself, as being a part of the whole then and only then things will change for the better.

If we are aware of our own personality, we may realize that there is much to learn about our ability, there is no reason to place ourselves in a limited situation or frame of doubts in our possibilities. One must focus only on constructive achievement.

The natural forces within us are the masters we should permit these forces to control. We must become excitement above the ordinary person of today, and dispose of the weak and doubtful perceptive thoughts about ourselves, which cause the limited achievement, which slows the unfolding of ones, true self.

Rid mankind of its shame a reflection of past and present fortune and mishaps in the world as we know have caused the unusual change in human nature. Being complex, the results of unharmonious has naturally expressed themselves in the channels where the disturbance occurred.

In riding mankind of its shame, and the achievement of respect for life, one is to rectify ones past mistakes, what I mean by change ones mistakes we know that one cannot undo or forget the past. But one can compel and forgive ourselves of the past acts. Just ask the Source of life to heal the past. The Divine Source who is the only Source for forgiveness of the past errors. We in turn are to be more mindful of one's future activities.

Since we wonder why and how the issues and events developed in our lives, we only seek the answers through accepted of what will be reviled.

Without a search within ourselves no clue will be found, unless understanding of ones own situation, most of the times we are the creator of our own conditions we are our own results, developed over many lifetimes. We are not saying all acts done were of non-constructive nature. We must think about what we must do to receive that perfect mind, the Spiritual-Mind or our Divine-Mind, which calls for changes in thought patterns.

In our observation, we sometime see persons with deformed bodies, or ones with disease working to destroy their-bodies, still through it all you find a refined disposition, in some of them one of compassion and with all the good qualities, you would think a person with good hearth and no physical challenges to confront them they would show good qualities in their character, not so for many are just the opposite many complain all the time about this or that is not right. There're some who have perfect bodies shaped in beauty, but seem to be determine to destroy and dishonor their bodies as nothing of importance, and with a selfish disposition.

Often we see the ones with beautiful nature and refinement are the ones who have evolved to a level through cleaning out their non-constructive karma, and working towards the Spiritual-Mind set or the Divine-Mind, in service to humanity, and have concerns for all life on the planet.

When the respect for life and the removal of mankind shame is achieved by the majority then the evolutional cycle in mankind consciousness, will be one of divine origin, and a new age will unfold for humanity, and the wheel of rebirth no longer will be needed. Our destiny is written in the stars of the universe.

As the respect and shame is brought into the light a clear path will form; life is light and light it life and all is Love, we all must be filled with the light of Love that gives all life.

There are higher and lower potentialities, one is fortunate to choose awareness and resolves to their own higher nature.

But until one accept the truth about the lower mind, which control ones activities, many times one may find themselves using this mind in wrong ways before they have learned to be conscious of this mind in what it does, accept its working and change the thought patters and become harmony with all life, not just humans, but all life on the planet in using this mind, remember you have the control by being conscious of it.

The invisible evils are the actions of mankind, refusing to come in alignment with the laws, which govern life. The offspring's of mankind creations are repeating the old patterns and we are becoming overwhelmed with wrong decision making, causing mental and physical torment, with over-kill in suffering.

We see that a seed develops into a tree and we follow the step in the process to full production of that seed to the tree, but when it comes to mankind we fail to determine or discover the appreciation for the principle development of mankind.

Mankind composition is the same it goes through a process like the tree although we haven't really discovery how a tree came out of a seed, we know that genes and chromosomes are the cause of the transmission; we still do not know or have not discovered how psychological characteristics can be contained and transmitted in the in conceit material vehicle. We do not see or know, but it is an expounded to us as a cogent of nature-process which is a performance of nature through electron, atoms, molecules, cells, glands, chemical secretions and physiological processed.

All the earth inhabitants are developed by their nature of existence although develop of different in species or forms, but all are the same created for different purposes. The original produce of life such as the cosmic magician automatically successfully produced the composition for all things in the highest quality.

As mankind started to use what is called "free Will or Choice." Things were altered for all of life on the earth, which caused a dramatic change in the true purpose of each species of life and their energy substances. This "free will" in originality was for the purpose of humankind to hold their attention of the consciousness fixed on the Divine Presence or principle of activity that at all times compels the upward flow of the energy. The moment any thought enters the mind that is not in harmony one can command it to change and be regulated back to the upward flow of Divine principle.

Our mistake is in trying to define life by our intelligence, it's not enough to describe life from our small intellect we must include the exclusive working of the Absolute. When one is face to face with all the shame, of past activity during the early part of our history, we must take responsibility for our actions which caused the problems we are trying to work through now in our present state. It is time to change the present and receive the splendor of the future. By transforming our minds realizing hatred brings more challenging situations in one's life.

We must take the opportunity to develop the higher consciousness and respect for all life to change the outcome in our future for humanity and all living things on this planet. We are inseparable, we all are linked together in our existence to be productive and all have the right to earn values, to increase the integration of the creations on this planet in rendering ultimate orchestration of unity for all.

We must stop being value destroyers and consumers of violations against the law of life. If humanity is to serve or should I say life on planet earth to serve we all must be honest about the conditions of life knowing it depend on us, our mind and efforts we make for survival of all life.

We as individuals are considered a fine piece of art, the production of a great work, by the Source of life, we are not an illusion, and only the conditions that humankind creates the deception and evilness are what blind the true good. We are surrounded with substance of greatness and that substance is within us, it's good. When you have come to the understand, you are great, and recognize the greatness as being the artwork of the Greatest of all and knowing without right activity from that Source of greatness there is nothing at all which creates it.

And So It Is

I am a being created by the Source of Life as a child of the Divine origin to live my purpose in peace and harmony with all life.

I am open to that Source to give me Divine inspiration to write with substance hopefully to assist in changing conditions in our world with the help of all of humanity, to open to the real power, the power which is "LOVE" for all life.

The word's comes from within my heart channeled by devotion to life, which is mine to command with the flame of love for all of life.

I am projecting my love throughout the world to every corner and shallow place which needs the light of truth, and love.

I am sending love to all life forms everywhere in all directions to perform the perfect work of the Source which has created us all and to return to me with all the divine Love and good, which I am sending forth. "And So Be It".

I am hopeful that this writing will assist mankind to eradicate the errors and break down the barriers of injustice and harmful acts which cause separation of all forms of life.

Beloved ones fill the circle of our world with mental and spiritual, love and peace. Be an out pouring of the active flame expanding out into all. We do embrace all things which mankind desires the necessary for ones highest – self to illuminate and become fully expressed in us knowing, there are three things, which are necessary, ones health, sufficient supply and love, those are ones attachments for living and to be happy that which fills all with the abundant life,.

PAST KARMA

Karma, a word comes from the Sanskrit meaning "to do; "to act." A word most frequently used to designate what may be called the effect or result of actions and the law of retribution, the ultimate law of the universe. It seems to be one of the best conceptual doctrines, which explains the meaning of the human attachments.

Karma is one of the words that many associate non-constructive activity, which cause life perhaps more pain then pleasure in its conditions, but many are not seeing the whole picture, Karma can be good as well as bad, its just action reflecting the real effects, which follow thoughts, and the actions, resulting a manifestation transformed. The aspects of the law of cause and effect, it's a principle of action and reaction, and the law of consequences. The mistaken idea that Karma somehow involves the concept of punishment that's "UNTRUE." We create conditions for our own punishment by our own actions.

To understand Karma more clearly, some believe an entity or judgmental higher throne past judgment on our activities and karma is the form of activity that brings only non-constructive results of an action of individuals, not so, it's not only disapproval it's a process which arises from all acts whether non-constructive or constructive or even neutral.

There is a word sound like the word Karma, this word is Kama — meaning self-indulgence is a misnomer in reality it should be called animal indulgences, Kama is the level of the animal which robs one of one's divinity, by all types of over gratifications. One is sexual degradation (that is, sexual activity without true love or without true concern for yourself or chosen partner at the time; Other form of over-indulgences, alcohol, tobacco habit, drug addiction, and food over-indulgences, also useless, aimless, laziness pastimes, habits which has no known real purpose in improvements of ones life.

Back to Karma, when a person who perform good deeds a change within that person will vibration- energy which will attract, the various envelopes and bodies of that individual, she or he will reap the result in a positive change for good, which aligns one with the positive forces.

The human condition is not the only ones effected by karma, it takes in all kingdoms, animals, plants, etc., all livings things develop karma, because all things evolves from one level to another, it is one of the tools for the cycle of evolution in life itself.

From the creative event of life of all things, there has been karma in existence, just as the elements have been, so have karma creation has unfolds itself as a system, which unfolds all of life creative plans and or laws.

We as humans must be concern with not only ones personal individual karma, but also ones social and nation etc. We see all around us those who disappoint us and ones who are disappointed and struggling with unfavorable conditions of their home, and social life and many with their environment, without a clue, of the reasons they're in the situation they are in. There are few people who have not, under certain circumstances, experienced the extension of their everyday boundaries. There are many who leap beyond the limits of one's exclusive human existence.

We carry the burden of ones social enslavement and ones nation and oneself, the constant thoughts and activity of nations and the development of social influences of individuals are holding many in captive positions.

Since the rising of mankind above the rest of the earth inhabitants, humans, come to believe they are above all other creatures, because of their ability to think and reason in a situation, but many of our humans show just the opposite, if they are who they believe they are, then why are their experiences not in proportion to the times? Humans are still behind in their development towards the Highest Consciousness, and they do not understand they are a part of the whole, but there are special ones called in this universe, although described special through experiences they have not confirm that they have evolved beyond other inhabitants.

All creation being linked is still seem to be a mystery to the insight of the average individual, they are not arriving to the ultimate reality through the process of investigation into the mysteries of life by looking within themselves first.

Humans are to evolve to the supreme intellect as permitted.

Many are claiming to be very religious or spiritual, yet their minds are not focus to realize the true purpose of one of character depictures persons of love with in ones heart is of one reality, which unifies life, that's love, harmony within self and being at peace with all living things is required.

With the supreme intelligence one can gain the primer purpose in fulfilling unity of life relatively speaking.

Past, as the manifestation of each moment becomes that moment of the past, each moment fulfill that moment, not looking back or to the start, the mystical insight will not penetrate beyond the barrier of that moment, which hides the past in that moment.

We are in mental evolutional transition; the old thinking must change in order for us to evolve to higher realms of enfoldment. Many of our societies are overlooking the need for serious question of the activities of the past. All of nature follows the same course cycles or repetitive activities, not really changing.

If we find insight into self-knowledge and the nature of good and evil, which causes karma to exist one will unfold to a higher- plane(path) for one's life. As one seek the good for all of humanity one learns the reason why and how to cause change. As we search and test the concerns to improve society, we can successfully develop the insight to constitute our future intellectual heritage.

Unfortunately mankind is habitably repeating the same mistakes down through the ages, not addressing the reasons why or how we come to this state. Knowing we must direct our attention to re-examine and analysis the unpardonable conditions and the self-deceptive attitude.

Many refuse to accept the fact they are the ones who are incapable of unsparing self-knowledge. Without commitment to the survival of mankind, civilization as we hope in the future it will be only a dream.

Civilization track record holds a lot to be desired, some may wonder why the need or concerns, if we are destine to fail. With the thought that people will not come together on the simplest things in life, why would I think this enormous issue would be different?

The past is a vast sounding board with the potentiality for good changes, but depend on the waves of sound giving direction to the impulses of the present it will be slow in completion. Yes, the revolution of materialism and intellect processed is a cycle, which causes mankind to focus more on these things, knowing in time will decay and be lost, not allowing one to be giving into ones potential for greatness, yes mankind has descended and reach the lowest point of mankind underdevelopment, but there is a chance.

There is a law in nature that operates in every area whether physical, or energy, which mankind can be assured will assist in the long run. Nature never creates the smallest or the most insignificant form without some definite purpose and use. We all are in the stages of evolving where everything and situation runs its course or cycle.

We live in a world, which is, governed by the realm of laws, and these laws cannot be broken.

Yet when the facts are recognized mankind hides from these laws, there is no hiding place one can go, the laws surround us. We live in a physical and mortal world since mankind is helpless, to these natural laws, why not obey them?

Having realized the relationship between man and nature, and the molding energies of the mind, which create ones destiny, Humankind seems to be trying to escape.

The search for the truth of the reasons why?

People generate a large number of destructive characters in thought-form, and thought form is acted upon and a huge mass of energy is precipitated on the physical plane, stirring up wars and social disturbances, resulting in collective non-constructive karma. There are those who believe one can change the activity of non-constructive karma into a form of grace, just by changing one's mind to good thoughts and not continuous feeding the memory of what has been in the past.

We must be conscious of the past not continue in the activity of that past to make change. I believe this is wishful thinking the point some are overlooking is everything must run its course, the past must be clean up if there is non-constructive karma, and if there is good a continuous built on to this good karma to receive that grace part one belief to be the golden gift. One cannot change the past only receive forgiveness for what's past, the changes come in the present and to develop the future.

A careful study of history and life's issues will show the numerous efforts of the wise ones, searching for solutions to mankind problems change within individually better. Although through the ages the searchers and seers develop sources of materials in the form of Ancient Philosophy, Sciences, Religions and other literature, which brought society from barbarism to civilize activities in order to guide humankind along in the stages or cycles of evolution.

It's been said, that we derive all of our principles from the Monad, being ones (spiritual intelligent substance). So as we realize that just as we derive our physical energy indirectly from the sun, we also derive our spiritual intellect or energies from the universal nature to teach others of mankind their glorious destiny.

Society is taking one step forward in the sciences and two steps backward in morality and compassion. The knowledge in the sciences is moving forward in various areas through the natural forces and phenomena, so what is missing?

The changes are slower than necessary to come as we should and the causes are those steps forward and backward. This is only because mankind, refuse to obey the laws in place, only have adapted themselves to the shame and clothes themselves in garments of degenerate and unethical-shameful activities of hatred, deception, and numerous acts of unpleasantness, which destructs the memory of the Universal-spark of mankind.

What is missing, progress as it could be; life accomplishments in the materiality area are not enough, to bring humankind to its full potential. Life is a project a business each individual on their own should be active in workout in their own lives. We must think of ourselves as an entrepreneur laying out the plans for the project for the most sensational outcome.

There are opinions where people think it's important to remember the past lives. I think It's not important in a sense to know the actual lives we have lived, reason being, we permit ourselves to enter the past allow those events to effect the present and maybe the future, the actual events are not important. The only things importance is how to apologize and ask for forgiveness for the unworthy deeds one has created in ones own past. If need be focus your concerns on yourselves in the present life with the thought of building good karma in the present for the future.

For society to open the door to success in the present for the future one must awaken and clear up the early part of this present life, all unnecessary loads from previous lives experiences, can be freed in ones mind by forgiveness of self first and ascend to a higher level, you may think what about the past, is she said to forget the past? You may be wondering, but if you don't know the past how can you correct it; The idea is to be open to whatever it is that needs to be corrected without knowing we do not know every mistake we made in this present life, so why do you think you will remember the past? The only way is to be open to positive changes, by infecting the human consciousness with new positive ways that is beneficial to all of mankind not only for oneself. Just perhaps mankind will clean the non-constructive karma out of the books of one's life and stop the wheel of rebirth.

In the past people were just fitting in, and were trap by the society of their birth, without concerns or motivation to the wonders of this universe, and living an ordinary life with ordinary standards for living. Every thought, every action were put in motion by ones desires or needs, and if these ideas became activities, we bought about the law of cause and effect, meaning karma.

The ultimate aim is to live conscious of the need to perfect ourselves and be the best-we can be and learn the lessons in life that is required of us for this time of experiences in the quest for completeness.

Civilization will advance significantly by change in character of the old thought system of the past knowing mankind survival depends on change.

Now let us reflect on some of the events and reasons which I think has prolong our inability for achievement of self-mastery

Let point in the right direction, who is taking observation of what is happing to the people of today?

To understand the profound difference between the standards of morality and what motivates a person to act as they do, one must product objectivity of reality rather than production of changeable standards of the times.

Materialism plays a part in most of the decisions we make and people usually are animated with any action that benefits their life style, desires, needs, even if it morally good or wrong hopefully no harm comes in with the activity and to the situation.

REFLECTION

Humankind in general is like tares in the field of life not understand still cannot fully understand the universe, and the answers are sowed to its meaning are puzzling and beyond ones intellectual grasp. The good thing is we who have enough sense know to gather the tare and burn them in the fire of truth and we seek explanations from the true Source of all good things.

As we bring these puzzling thoughts into focus the answers do come bringing the puzzle pieces together for development for us to master ourselves and hopefully become that image required by our Creator.

First of-all this is not an act of being judgmental or a form of self-righteous opinion it's only to get many to look beyond oneself-egotism.

Let's explain one thing, we sometime use one word for different things and this will lead to missing the true meaning of that word, and in ancient time they used more than one word for the same thing but the people of yesterday and today use one word for different meaning for example the Bible the Original One take the word "life," there are people with the idea that we have one body and one so-call lifetime, but we have non-stop existence in many forms, wherein others do believe there are many lifetimes and it come to all believe in some kind of continuous of non-stop life.

In reality both are right to a point; think about this, we all believe in a spectacular universal entity of some kind that control all that exist, why not go a step further; All of the Universities are govern by their perspective relative "Life," and we all are a part of that "One Life," there not a so-call "nothing" until that polluted entity in its form of life refuse in its allotted time to come to evolvement of its purpose, although most entities usually use the time wisely because they know it's more than this form of life and all is life, relative speaking, everything has its purpose and most things are unknown to us on or in this little spot of the unknown, this is why we understand so little of the worlds around us, because the average person are not explorers into the mysteries of our existence. We can learn many things through our minds when we let the Supreme-Mind Power of Life to open our minds to those things one seek to know, it's all about the mind-set of the individual.

Humankind activities of the past and present is based on their growth or lack of in a conscious state of practice and use of one's power by mandating their impulses, emotions, thoughts, and impersonal desires to bring the quality of one's life, knowing all depend on the level ones conscious mind-set or rest at the time.

Every thought every action that we have sets in motion a cause and produce karma and the effects can be beneficial or unfavorable, as we live and breathe from moment to moment, we are shaping our destiny and our karma.

What can we do, when our nation is causing unfavorable conditions and causing bad karma, which is distance or impersonal to you as an individual?

There it a question to be addressed, are we as members of a nation responsible for the decisions of our so-call leaders? Should we carry the burden of those leaders' decisions in our personal karma, reaping the work of the hands of that taskmaster?

Yes, in my opinion we must take some responsibility, I guess you are wondering why? That's a long story, but will be given in brief. To say, we made the decision to permit this person to represent us. When the veil is removed about the leader has done his dirt work it's to last, but as individuals we can change things in the present, you as individuals can breaks through and realizes that there is activity in ones country that you must change, take the power of the people in voice to change things, by have become aware and you can help to change or control you must take some responsibility, now if you cannot influence the activities, for better changes than the law of cause and effect returns to the source who intimate the act it's their responsibility themselves, but also understand you chose the nation to which you came at the time of birth for whatever reason. That's another story. For whatever reason neither you nor I know, the complete reasons, it's a part of the individual development or enfoldment there are things beyond our conscious knowledge at the moment.

The organizational function of the universes are in place before ones entrance a given so-call new lifetime, you made a decision to where you wanted to be born, and the lessons to be learned in this new and present physical body. So there is no detachment from some of the events where we can become indifferent of its result in karma.

Persons who deliberately break the vow, lose control of the desired personality and the chase to receive the ultimate mastery of their selves and unable to enter the kingdom of deathlessness or stop rebirth. It takes self-mastering to break the wheel of rebirth.

When ones egocentric self-consciousness with its strong holds firmly to protect its psychological false nature, is in play many are gathering the illusive forces against the unwanted changes, their evolvement are being slowed down from their progression.

When ones personality reflex self-centered, deceptive and a defensive modes, one undertakes and perform activities of life restriction rather than life enhancements, by resisting ones nobler impulsive nature, choosing ignorance over knowledge of what is required of mankind, then one must accept the results and that could mean wrong (bad) karma.

Crisis

When every aspect of a person life is to "get you before one get me" is one's mind frame and to be deceptive toward others causes a breakdown of society. We as humans are not evolved enough as we could be, the time is running –out on societies the animals are moving pass the humans in their purpose.

Humans are so engaged in deceptive activity that the thought of doing a good act is beyond their so-call rational mind's, understand I am not speaking of all of humans, because there are many builders of societies, virtuous ones, people that are genuinely good and show true love in their hearts for others in this world. There are others show the opposite, they do not know what it is to be an example of kindness. These are the ones who are misusing others for personal material gain, not understanding things change, that saying, "here today gone tomorrow," nothing remains the same over time changes come to us in the form of lessons, the purpose of these lessons is for our learning and the result of the thought-process downward spiral which creates conditions to continuing that downward spiral.

Humankind activities reflects ones growth or the lack of by ones impulse, emotions, thoughts or impersonal concerns of self and others, the motives and quality of activity are depending on the level of one's conscious-mind rest.

However the deluded mind tends to become increasingly conditioned and restricted by habits and memories of its perceptions and experiences, although one is aware of their ego-centered desires, it may be difficult to overcome when the desire is strong and others influences reinforces that type of activity.

It is characteristic of mankind to be confused whether to do right or wrong, if both ways seem to payoff in what the individual wants. Although the results show itself later in this life or the next, the results of its making may not be to ones liking.

The qualities of mankind nature, is described in the history books, memories of past conditions of suffering and torment.

We have had many highly evolved enlighten individuals in the past and present, which are making a difference in the quality of life for many individuals. These highly enlighten persons are working from their Higher- center, which sends impulses to affect all of nature, offering a noble service.

Since the development of mind, the brain became conscious of itself and its function, mankind have made decisions for themselves, in doing so, the undeveloped individual who's consciousness is basically focus on the uncertainty and vacillating intermediate nature are restless, with the thought of one's own self-preservation, understandable in a way, but not understandable in another, we are a part of the whole.

While striving for self-preservation and what we deem to be desirable, the record is being made relating to ones contributions or annihilations.

Every person is a soul expression though a mind and personality, although many seem to forget their purpose, there is an inner level within their being (spirit) that holds the keys to the answers to life.

But many human endeavors are to rid the mind of the responsibility of their actions. Most people do not sincerely desire criticism, and aspire to unfold their greater side of their nature. Many are still in denial and refuse to accept their divine part of themselves. They restrict the influences that will enable them to experience the truth of themselves and to become self-realized.

The outer mind through long periods of time habit has given enormous power and authority to control our evolvement, not saying all individuals have limited themselves, understand no outer thing has any power in ones experience, except what a person give by feeding into it.

Our success in life is based on removal of the delusion and illusions that prevail in the mind, which stops the awareness. When the mind becomes illumined with light, the Source of existence will spontaneously reveal ones true self to the individual.

By giving this great Higher Presence within all power to do the things one require the individual allows himself or herself to call on the law of forgiveness to direct the energy of that law to grant one the mastership of self, that will correct and adjust the wrongs; and one will accomplish the true freedom, and all their future conquest will be a breeze.

When we become the master of ourselves and receive the Highest-Awareness, we no longer can be disturbed by the outer conditions, not because of disinterest, but the result of understanding, which makes one receptive to divine intervention it will illumine ones consciousness.

Most human's activities are useless for real growth in areas that will make them master of their selves and not really productive, in they are just something to do, and their attention is focus on foolishness.

Although we are in a timeless law of nature and or universe, we should make life worthwhile and know what is required to transform into one of pure aspiration of an awaken soul.

Since the principles are for caution and to support harmonious process in our expression of enfoldment in consciousness of the higher self affect through our evolution process. Humankind behavior and mental state should progress and transform to create a self-discipline personality, which would receive the benefits to be that ideal individual.

The Creative Source of the manifested universe and all within it knows all wonders in our condition, what causes and what it takes to correct it. The Creator of Life know what happen in each one of us in our past lives, which cause the present state to be as it is, and also know what the future holds if conditions are not changed for the better, and What and why a continuous of rebirths to the same condition at present. It all boils down to the activity of change for improvement of one's individual mode.

When the individual cannot look beyond their material being(the body), which conditions the soul for the repetition of birth and death in the physical form, that person manifest the energy which produces limited potencies, by being under the influence of such potency one become condition by the three modes of one's nature, food, shelter, and defense.

Humankind is generally wasting the very energy that reinforces and strength the link between the Universal-Head and oneself. As individuals the life force holds fast, when the outer self-use the life's energy to create wrong conditions the wasted energy becomes non-productive and drain on the potency for the advance of one's consciousness.

It all boils down to humankind and his free will, the more conscious he becomes of the fact of being able to create at will, he put effort in the direction to benefits oneself, and perhaps towards what is noble or ignoble and thus one becomes beautiful or ugly in ones character.

Humankind have burden itself with impurity in the form of matter and ones emotional world, the gratification of the physical appetites and the material comforts, remain unrecognized as problems, and more and more the great truths are being over looked. Not saying some of these things are not good, everyone wants comfort of a good life, the problem is how far one goes to have them. Until mankind cast off the burden and redeem itself, there will always be confusion and dissatisfaction in ones real link to ones Higher- part.

From the beginning free will has existed, but because of the choices we have made in the past we have develop the non-productive karma as well as good so to redeem ourselves from the wrong choices of the past, we must correct errors in the present. This free will has caused many to be burden to great attachment of wrong karma and they cannot see their way out.

Humankind has placed the blame and so-call injustice lies in the unequal circumstances in ones birthplace or family conditions and one being born burdened with a hereditary disease, and just maybe the child is bearing the errors of the parents or family or one can be totally innocent of the wrongs to be far them, but most of the time its our burdened are our own, perhaps the condition is for others reasons, learning and you became the instrument?

We see the difficulty in believing there is justice and when the system cannot comprehend the action of those persons in this period and in the past, which could have been by pre-ordained of karmic law. There are historically data in one's life-story, yes we are all in the evolutional stages of one's personal consciousness and each individual does not work out their human progress the same time or way.

The whole of civilizations are not alike, in evolvement each individual is specially organized reaches the same level of attainment in different ways and times, perhaps the same or other geological strata. In different parts of the globe people culture are different and their belief system is different, some are more primitive in mind and in their environmental conditions, even now in this time of modern technology some are still cave-dwellers.

It's perfectly normal to wonder why some flourish and others are in poverty, seem to fade away. The mystery of one's birth strata is not difficult to understand, if one realized, when mankind started out on his course in their life's he stood free of karma or fade attached to him, a clear and clean record, only when one became the authoritarian of that free will to chose a path for good or evil did the downhill movement occur in its beginning. In securing a path towards the good or the conditions that brings non-productive karma is ones chose.

As mankind shapes one's own future experiences of life, it brings us to the stage we are now, one can prevent more of the same in this time of events and stop the past from continually control or one be determine to change the conditions in which ones soul has been born for new type of influences that would be beneficial during the earthly stay in this new physical body.

Normally, when a body is cast- off a need for a new one of that particular soul needs molding, to casting off non-productive karma, for the future development.

With each incarnation one brings past non-productive and productive karma if not a higher level is developed in the present incarnation, one will not shake off the past karma it will recurs in every lifetime until the non-productive karma it loses its strong-hold, knowing in the present it seems to be stronger than mankind true spirit for goodness to overcome the past.

If humans, fail to remove the non-productive karma in their individual lifetimes the progress will be slow to reach ones full potential to be a higher-spiritual being within.

The important thing for mankind to understand, is that what he plants, he will harvest and in following the path of redemption and creating good karma in time it will bring a certain measure of purity for them as individuals, which will naturally be reflected in ones deeds.

If humans would not be entirely absorbed in everyday life and entertainment and pay attention to what's happening around them to a point, and seeing their needs will change for the better in their activity toward each other in the form of unity in love for humanity as a whole, one would be less in tears of sorrow for the lack of development of humanity.

The true expression of mankind is to humble oneself toward the will of one's Creative Source and have respect for each creature created by that Higher Creative Source.

Humans should think be conscious and submit to humility and to the will of one's Creator by having respect for the laws in place for our good, every happening is created by a cause, and the operation of karma can never be completed, so one can received the redemption to be enforced in humankind, respect for the laws in nature directed by the Higher Powers.

The most important thing was save for last, it is the "how" to reclaim one's rightful place and be accepted as one who mastered the wrong and bad influences that causes one to return to earth plane repeating over and over the same activities, until one decide to change.

The explanation for constant return is that one doesn't transmute or erase past karma that is wrong, to free oneself from the wheel of rebirth. I guess you are wondering how one can do this.

The law of forgiveness of self and others that has brought bad events in your lives from one's very existence as being an entity sent to the earth plane.

The law of forgiveness is a large subject I think we all understand the bases in the law. One forgives by wiping the slate clean or one can say let off the hook pardon if you will and having mercy, in regard to others, but one must also forgive oneself. In forgiving oneself that means to master oneself and reframe from of all wrong activities, which

Has brought you to the place on the evolved plane in which you are now standing. Self-forgiveness is to be accepted, without judgment that we are in the moment, our weaknesses and our strong points as well. We cannot undo the past it's done, but we can forgive the past by showing mercy toward ourselves and ask for forgiveness from our Source- Creator. We cannot see beyond the veil of this present life to read the karmic record, only in dreams or the physic, some come through hypnotic regression, but there is a drawback in the regression excises, one may receive all kinds of memories and thoughts and may not be your own, which can cause confusion of what is really your own experiences in the different lifetimes in which you have lived.

In seeking forgiveness one must use at least two methods; one asks for forgiveness of the past wrong karma, by using spiritual decrees. Two,

Take time out each day regularly maybe three times in a day in reinforce the thought into the mind or subconscious by give decrees.

Understand it makes no different in ones type of spiritual systems or philosophy the purpose is the same to change the karma seeds to balance ones current life challenges which will broke the karma cycle of the past. Whatever spiritual level one may find oneself, there is an energy vibration that surrounds your being, the more spiritual one becomes the more powerful the energy and one is unlikely to be motivated to act in activities of wrong, which can slow ones evolvement.

To provide some of the information's I myself use it could be useful to you as-well. First I call forth the white light or the cosmic light for protection, then I meditated on what I think is required for me as an individual to make the Omnipresent and the Light and the God Substance come full-force in my life to steadily rise my being into the Mighty Perfection where I am free from all sense of limitations from the non-constructive activity and desires.

I believe all of humanity needs the firm consciousness of one's Deity, myself I focus on my beloved I Am Presence of God Presence within me to direct my every movement. I ask for forgiveness each and every day for things I may have done without being conscious of or knowing and to cleanse my past karma from past lifetimes, by using the Violet transmuting flame.

You may be wondering what's the violet flame, now that is a whole new subject which is to extensive to speak on right now. I will say this, it works like a detergent using positive and negative charges of atoms, it works on each molecule knowing there are two sides the positive and negative, what people do not understand that positive and negative both are good, here are again using words we don't understand to the fullness. Let me explain, positive energy and negative energy is what make things work in balance, the universe, and even the elements have positive and negative vibrating forces.

Back to invoking the violet flame it sets up a polarity between matter and spirit, the nucleus of the atom which is the negative pole and spirit the positive pole interact causes the light in the violet flame to establish an oscillation to dislodge past activity that is trapped between the electrons orbiting the nucleus of the atoms.

Unlike detergent leaving a soap firm, the violet-flame it not only surround the debris, it transforms into pure positive light-energy causing ones freedom and raises ones vibration to move one into a more spiritual level.

Decrees:

"Beloved I Am Presence of God listen to my plea for forgiveness, only thee will I direct my heart and mind open to thy will."

"Lift me in the light of your Mighty Presence, the Great I AM Presence and in the Love which only comes from you."
And So It Is"

"Beloved Mighty I Am Presence of God, now you fully consume and prequalify all my energy that would slow my evolvement. "And So It Is"

You can develop your own decrees or prayers to direct your deities and change the energy for your presence life, along with working on your past karma in other lifetimes that has been what call wrong or non-constructive. As we think or act, our personal mind travel into the universal mind which causes a chain reaction to create good or the opposite for one's life.

As you give, so shall you receive, it's the law of nature. In truth you are giving and sharing your most desire for yourself for the small-less act or thought is an extension of yourself, this is why one must be mindful of one's thoughts, because they create.

It's like each and every time one think a good or positive thought about something it immediately follow with a good feeling about it, and when you follow it up with words it enforces a kind of power that set in motion into one's subconscious mind for spreading It's roots over your entire being for good.

Be open to creative thoughts and or inspiration as long as it not harmful to others and to other forms of life. Life must be respected, in truth we humans do not give or create the forms of matter which is life, only one form of life comes though us and that's human only, but we do not create the substance in its origination.

We are permitted to create activities that to our wishes as for our own life, because we have the use of "free will or choice" for the course of our lives.

"Ultimate Liberation from the Wheel of Rebirth"

NATIONS IMPACT WITH TABOOS

Deep-rooted taboos are worldwide; the spontaneous response to the cultures of different nations in their inherent is recorded throughout history.

Undeveloped man has always stood in awe of the mysteries in life, so he made his own rules in how he will live life. All speculation concerning life has been futile to those who made their own rules.

Question, do we understand the purpose for which we were created? Perhaps the goal was to awaken the substance of matter to the ultimate energy of spirit, as it manifests itself in the divination of the Godhead toward the perfect nests of truth in matter.

The average individual is mixed with taboos, and feels justified for their point of view. They assert their experiences to support their logic using the physical senses, which they are themselves, unable to perceive anything immaterial or not organized as gross matter.

There is a beyond, the form of matter, a consciousness, we call the Cosmic Consciousness and it's obtainable to us in only the relative sense one has to reach Spiritual-Consciousness first. The physical world is only frame for our experiences, and the senses are our instruments, to function on this physical plane... To go beyond the matter and senses, one must become self-realized and observe the witnesses of the world in other fields of manifestation and instruments at work with substance beyond the matter of this world which works harmoniously in the other forms of substance. The appearances are real, the rhythm of the universe and their counterparts works together as a whole.

We need not give up the bodily life to obtain the in-sight of the beyond, only change our way of perceiving life. Our feelings and emotions are responsive what we think and to what goes on in our world, and most of all in our nation, which rules out, survival.

The destiny of humankind is only one part of the wholes plan; we as humans are not the only ones evolving in these universes. The planets and all, which inhabits of the earth and elsewhere, are in the plan too.

We must see the true relations of all inhabit, because of those who are engage in wrong activities thinks, it's okay, have become illusively worse, we must remove the veil of ignorance that hold many in its illusion.

We do not become perfect by shifting from one side to another as the wind blow, one day think one way and tomorrow another and another and another it shows an imperfect attainment to limited attributes. In no way one should abandon progressive altitudes and constructive improvement.

There is an element of error in humankind many are not self-conscious of their true creative power or their free will, or choices, without understanding that doubts and fears are unnatural causes one to become unbalance narrow and limited.

Our experiences which will cause an expanding of self-conscious can be sensed by the presence of the contact with a form of intelligence far in advance of our own.

But knowledge in general is really what is unavoidable, and that's a different story. We as individuals will to think and create at will ones experiences in life. Basely on the attribute developed over time, perhaps in other life-times, it still the creative power of the Divine Source working in us carried over from the past.

Since humans, individually are evolving on different levels in different times; it's hard to group, similarly because our will and many being ignorant of the rest, has fallen into error slowing one's development, the knowledge of a greater or less degree of incapacity impotence is affecting all to some degree.

Different nations have different ideas about how their nation should be govern and developed. Individuals are born in these nations according to their level of growth or need for lessons to be learned in that given lifetime, also there are persons born in areas to teach other individual's the truth about life and its purpose. There is also an inner meaning to all experiences in life the radiance of consciousness can be perceived by ones spiritual eye, which energizes the mind, giving one the awareness to unfold, through love, wisdom and constructive power in activity.

We don't always have a choice about some changes; sometimes it's forced on us by the decision of others who touch our lives. The nations governmental system, friends, parents, teachers, employers and whoever speaks to us through daily contact, creates ones thought system in times of contact.

When we go outside of ourselves and observe our lives and our endeavors, we soon find almost our whole life of activities are based on action and desires with the existence of others. Have you notice that our whole nature resembles that of socialists? We eat food that others have assisted in its production and wear clothes that others have made and live in houses that others have built, but we still feel a sense of impersonal to these persons, not understand they are working not only for a wage, but for your comfort and security.

And if they do not use quality material and craftsmanship in their work then they are unworthy of your confidence. People must understand that they have a great responsibility to show worthiness in promotion of all certain goals and values of objectives one may attain agree too.

Can nations leaders of the world come to the point of ensuring the future for all of mankind or should I say of all living creatures on the planet earth?

Since the discovery of nuclear warfare the chain reaction around the world in all nations leader mind, "I must have that which to warrant off my enemies," who is your enemies? It can be your own leaders, with that evil in their minds as well as others mind, persons which will-not change because of the thought losing power over the people or other countries or just out of fear. But, some nations do not have the control, nor should I say the mental stuff to control their anger, or addictions for power. Their leaders have not learned how to escape emotional sensitive response, which impact their people and the events that are necessary to keep each one of us alive.

The progress in science and technology is getting stronger each day is appreciated by every person who encounters the technical application of these sciences, nevertheless its achievement of science will not override the human need that only another human being can give. Technology cannot receive sensitizes of life as we can gain from one another. Although these things are important, we cannot achieve strength, courage, and confidence by superficial things, but we can by every experience, after one decide to move toward change from learning experience for change and start taking those first steps, it's the pleasures of life.

It reasonable to think in dealing with people of different backgrounds in the form of customs and traditions, we do not form a union in thought, even about the fate of mankind many see it differently, in how it could be, it certainly makes more sense to question which traditions are harmful and which are useful to the human beings in the long run.

All nations, people are crying for their independent, it's essential for a people to feel they are free, because it's been drummed into all societies from day one and rightfully so all are created equally not for males only, but also females as well to be equal to males all are human-beings. There was a time where the egoism stepped in to separate the genders, and the objective of the human plan was intoxicated with fear and tried to change the course of the human destiny. All mankind must learn and understand each fellow human-being are the same in makeup, as humans they all have the same needs and wants. Motives of each human being in their illusions and their suffering as well, we all have some value or moral system in play and some are good, and there are some of opposite in all nations.

There are nations, which enslave their people for different reasons, is doesn't make is right for whatever the reason. Unfortunately it's being accepted and tolerated as a way of life. The problem people fear change and the discomfort of looking forward to the changes of one's future. People in general feel safe in their habits, change bring one out of their confusion zone. A feeling of unsure and losing control take place and makes one fearful.

The different forms of slavery one can experience is not your everyday thoughts, but the underlining ones, like deception the stuff you don't look at as being wrong, because it's been done so long one overlook it. When someone takes your dreams causes you to feel hopeless and wonder, cause you to think what is wonderful about your life? You begin to accept this behavior as being befitting you. If anxiety is longevity and enough attention is placed on the activity it enforces and becomes a part of the individual accepted fate.

Just as some nations teach their young the doctrine of all forms of non-productive views and removing the children from their homes against their will endangering their minds with hatred, and selling them in the trade-market for slave activity in the form of general-labor, as house servants, in sweatshops, factories, plantations and in brothels as sex workers for others so-call physical pleasures knowing their activity is shameful toward humanity.

Because their countries are less fortunate economically then other countries, many non-moral acts are preformed and with the feelings that occur at those times in these individuals are shown in forms of anger, hopelessness, fear, disappointment, helplessness and most of all, they feel resentment for others more fortunate. Sometimes it takes years for them to understand other nations are not the blame for their nation conditions, maybe if they would open their eyes and see the injustice they are enduring to their own people is the cause? Understand I am not speaking of nations who wage wars against each other; within their nation, understandable both are not innocent.

It is not enough to teach mankind a specialty for physical maintains nests, it's important to teach one the basis moral and the virtues to unify humanity, most of all to the things which honors the principles for one to live by. We humans are in line to become gods, only if we see beyond the veil of humankind ignorance.

The whole drama in human's life is based on ones struggles between ones higher and lower nature, which is ones goodness and evilness that is centered round ones personality. And if ones nation is teaching violence in the form of hatred, deception and greed, and spend much of their time nursing their attitude that others are out to get them and to take what they have or who are not willing to assist them in their needs, they see others as their enemies.

In plans for the armament in different countries has taken the forefront in dealing with their views or opinion of other nations other than themselves, many are not seeing themselves as being their own problem in many cases. Yes, many have financial weaknesses, in their counties, which makes them feel anger and some of these countries with their insecurities face the future with despondency not knowing if they are going to survive as a nation because of their financial inadequateness, afraid of being taken over by nations with tremendous financial power in all areas, this causes a certain amount of insecurity on the part of the weaker nations.

We know there are events that have cause some nations to be unable to support themselves by other nations stealing their natural resources.

The focus has been on armament in warfare between the nations and not against the armament against poverty, disease and hatred. We need to come up with ways to prevent wars, competitive armament is not a way to prevent war.

There is a simple solution to a peaceful condition between nation and that is to focus one's mind on peacefulness and love for each other as human beings, knowing we all have the same needs, wants, comfort and safety in mind and body.

There are human rights, as we become fully aware of the worlds situation, without love and peace for mankind of all races and colors there will be no unity of humanity, or world peace. Not only must we become aware of issues, but remember all humans are part of this vast universe and the essences of the supreme substance in creation.

We as humans are responsible for reasoning, being ones with the ability to use our minds individually. We are not like the kangaroo born in three weeks and crawl from one's mother's womb to a pouch; we have evolved from beyond the mammal's stage.

Although humans dependent on their second womb, the home or the parents biological innovation for many years to mature and receive basic social imprinting to be established. Through the parents or substitute advice one mature and becomes independent of that second womb.

The young human puts behind dependency and become responsible for all their actions, hopefully the psychological maturity has developed to support ones challenges in their environment. The first requirement of any society is that its adult members to establish a personal sentiment that will appropriate to the society in which one lives.

We know that culture must be one of the foundations for world unification and understanding. In order to grasp the significance of a must for unity of all people, maturity of mind must be in play. The effectiveness of ignorance or should, I say the lack of growth in understanding of what is required of mankind to enter that third womb of pure truth and light, which functions independently of our limited growth so far, we see the need for awareness of the devastation around the world, because of lack of growth in the peoples mind, they are feeding the lower part of their being, that part which has not evolved to the level of being the supreme image of one's true divinity.

It's understood that uniting nations with the same ideas and opinions, with the need for disarmament is a dream come true, but many refuse to be concern, with fears of being exploited economically by the more powerful nations. There are those who are fearful of the power lose within their own governing structure. By eliminating wars, one can be assured that peace worldwide will give political health for the people

Most of the world's leaders are really not concern with the people as a whole, in the form of survival, think about it, the need for population control, there are under-lining things, which are not talked about. In society people are over-looking many issues that are unspoken. For example take the issues of population control, there are nations who are refusing aid to other countries who are in need of simple birth control and or disease control, but these powerful nations who refuse to supply these small countries with proper aide to control different situations, the people are starving not just for food but just for an act of kindness, from people, because of their inability to feed their children and themselves, and disease is out of control this is the question, why are we letting them just dying. Some of the powerful nations waste billions of dollars on wars, but unwilling to assist people to live, out of fear of over-population, and to control other events that may affect them in a later date or are they just unconcern?

Can you see the "shame," buy and selling the moral image, being disobeyed to the law of creation. Sacrificing respect and devotion to ones fellowman, only to entertain, the thoughts of fear, and the idea all of the events will not haunt them, the dead are not coming back, and since death alone would be no punishment for them. Not so, there is a sentence for all crimes against all life, be assured it will be delivered. Whether, nation or individual one will reap the harvest of their labors good or evil.

Let's speak on another issue, highlighted in the media, trafficking of human beings for profit, it's estimated that 1.2 million children are taken from their homes against their will each year. Tragic is normal practice in major cities around the world, if you can call trafficking humans as normal. The governments of these nations do not really care, it's a way of life for them, besides it's a 10 billion multi-national industry, with is vast inter-connected underworld thriving in the new global marketplace.

I just want you to think about it, and really think if you are a part of this activity. Are you listening, if you were a victim of this type of wrongness, not your children, but you as an individual, were misused, abused, tortured and raped of your own dignity, how would you feel, knowing the shoes is on your foot, not someone else?

Shame, shame, shame, these are taboo's, these victim cannot say, what is wonderful about their lives, they are feeling hopeless, and have no control of their own future as long as people are so determine in their evilness to victimize others for profit.

The victims do not feel encourage dreaming for a better life, disappointed in the society in which they are born or moved too. Some are disappointed not only in their nation, but their families as well, in some cases their parents being their problem.

A strange thing, to think the parents could be the problem these are the ones who are given the charge to protect them from the bad ones. Yes there are times when the family is the problem.

Question, what are the qualities of a good family? Could it be caring, honesty, reliability, trustworthy, and sensibility to your needs and patient in weakens.

It is easy to see how such views arise out of one's observation of life even the most appeared desires have limits in choices at best. How many people do we know who are free?

The biggest personal loss in one's life is to lose respect for oneself, in harming others when they are at their weakest point, stop and ask yourself are these taboo's, then listen, invited truth in your mind and heart, feel free sometime to ask your victim, how they feel, don't ignored the asking or the answer, it may tell you something about you.

The infant has just begun to cry, its tongue is tender by being pushing away from nourishment, which keeps one alive; the offering of good has abandoned the child life.

Let us, turn directly to the big question. What are we going to do about these taboos and problems in our nations that need to rid mankind of its shame?

To live as an individual released of the human shame, one has to know how and why and when to put on and to put off masks of the various roles. Question ones judgment and moral values; also see if you are a part of the problems.

When a society is indoctrinated and brainwashed to believe their ways is the only way, and no one has the right to question their belief or view. These persons become as robots nothing other, nothing less and nothing more, one is in a controlled situation. The individual never comes to the knowledge of oneself as anything but the more or less competent robot of a perfectly standard part. Understand, you are not your body; you are not your ego, think of these as delusory.

To say this in being brief, nations around the world have their own thought systems, and it's difficult to get people to agree on issues that are important. Differs are wide spread, as we westerns take pride in our freedom, an individual is able to do what one wants, and when one wants to do it, and think what one wants, having one's own point-of –view, but it this a fully true thought about my nation, we have problems of mostly deception from some of our leaders. Whereas some nations will not permit their citizens to voice their views and the thought of freedom is mocha means freedom from every impulse to exist.

We return here to say something more about the individual personality. The whole drama of life is made up of struggles within oneself, which has spends over on others, and harms repeal through the centuries.

The personality is dual and it's the instrument that urges our actions developing will power, imagination, reason creative intellect and with the animal instinct and desire, resulting in ones personality becomes strong self-centered and demanding. It's two forces in the human nature the positive or spiritual and the negative or lower nature has been at war down through the ages.

Mankind higher and lower self with its disappointments and enable to follow through on ones dreams and being a failure in relationships, it's understand able to easily give up hope and at times feel of giving up on life, when there seem to be no way out of one's situation.

The truth of ourselves lies within and not on the surface, although others have effect on our lives, we live in a social world, and that causes problems with the different personalities and views, by touching others vibrations of pleasure, pain, indifferences, as so many are being superficial. For it is no longer a mere acceptance without subjection, the times are worse now.

We humans carry our own heaven or hell within our own world by the character we project in the activities we perform. If we disobey the laws of life, it will be like breaking a branch off of a tree in a storm. Humans generate chaos and distress by the false conceptions of survival. One believes that one must be a deceiver to be successful, only opportunity has the power for one to succeed.

Humankind has changed little since their arrival, although have had time to sufficiently achieve their equilibrium of moral appropriate season for the cycles of their destiny.

All nations have their various complete systems, which have professed but failed, incomplete but prevalent among all civilized peoples. They all practice agriculture; commercialism and they possess these arts with normal amount of sanity, and morality, that's not enough.

In their ambitions to grow in power their vision is clouded by their displacement, the leaders of many nations are practicing a thin line of deception. But the truth is only suffering and ignorance exists in the minds of those with that type of views of life.

So we see life for those individuals is a dynamic play of a universal force, a force in which the personality or mental consciousness and nervous vitality are in some form or at least in their principle always inherent and therefore they appear and organize themselves in the physical world as the forms of desires, with conflict of impulses.

Mostly non-constructive deeds are being nourished by various means, whether directly or indirectly by discharges of the physical emerging in its effort.

We can trace presently some of the conflicts and confusions in play, there are moral limits to seriousness and utter literalness in thought, in exploring their options, they come to discovery humankind is in the crossroad either to move forward to express the impulses to be selfish or unselfish in service of being honorable in civic or for nation betterment to give help and consolation to those in sorrow or needs.

The nations of the world have a responsibility, to stop furnishing the means for destruction of the human life and the humiliating slavery into which plungers the individual, who are unfortunate to live in nations that sanction slavery.

There is a ray of hope, with the few, which have the moral greatness to resist, causing them to become the heroes of that society to change the other statesmen, in the things of the mind. The victory or success as a mere acceptance to the changes in views, detach reception in the depths of their past and present habitual reaction to different issues and conditions. We must not be controlled by imperfection in values, being able to convert imperfect false into true values.

The bottom-line every fact and movement is free, and all nations have a choice to grow or stay ignorant to their responsibilities, all nations have codes or system which they follow. Since each movement and thought is free in positing in itself has a certain vehemence or will by which it not only exists but seems to enjoy existing and defy extinction. For one must understand the compulsion begins when free action is in one direction collides with free action in another. There is no logical necessity for nations to continue in the same bad habits, which will slow their progress.

The world is continually suffering for the lack of change, humankind in its refusal to and ignores the true process and progression involved in a moral change. Meantime, the continuous trick of adaptation to the old ways is twisting the life out of the present generation. There are some things should not be permitted, people have the right of personal private see, the sets of power (government) are not striking a balance with the people, in the communities, only when time to change persons in the power sets. They don't ask communities leader that bring people together for talk on what the needs are in those communities they only want votes to place them office, and permit the police to control the people, or and the other new agent so-call Homeland Security to violate people liberty or rights of private –see by surveillance on the streets and come into there homes with out warrant, saying we had a tip that some one in your home is a criminal, or they have the right to come in because "I am homeland security" and we represent the Government. In truth the government has restricted people's personal freedoms in the name of National Security by removing their rights of private.

Think about this; every single act in foreign policy is governed exclusively by its leaders viewpoint, they feel in order to achieve utmost superiority over their opponent is to wage war, whether economically or militarily and by controlling of its citizens through subjection to terror or mind control. They tell their citizens it's for national security that they are taking some disgraceful actions, but reality it's only financial power they are seeking.

Most national believe independent is a marvelous thing, no saying it's not, but there are other things we must be concern with and that's international cooperation, even in scientific research etc., No one nation has all the answers to the many questions facing Humanity.

All must devote their time to the common interest of humans as a whole. All demand, should not be only for strength the warfare but insight to the achievements of peace and quality in oneself, and the nations.

We, right-minded people must bring to the attention of those who are still looking back at the old ways of the betrayers of the sacred trust of humankind in showing love toward their fellowman as their selves. Humans can aid each other in great works to restore healthy societies around the world and some are doing it that is good but most are not even tiring.

All destructive authorities in every nation can be overcome and render powerless, if the people withdraw their support and say "no more," "We will not be victims of your insanity, with your power to plunder us with destruction of our values and mortality for all of humankind.

Culture understanding it's a must for the world to unite with understanding, although, we have a United Nations Organization, all nations are not properly represented in this group. There are nations I believe are still refusing and object to the organization.

We all have a meeting of the minds because our prime concern is for the development of all mankind, the productiveness of all people surpasses all disagreements, we must escape the old feelings of jealous, inadequate, and disappointment in another nation, and let it be in the past, create a productive future. Be still being caution, one must but not be overly concerned where it will lead hopefully you experience a normal relationship with other people.

We may not realize we are the same as far as needs and feelings, although some may not be able to express their feelings because of their background are not simply as your people response differently to one thing, and feeling in different ways.

People who have different backgrounds are not always able to identify and express what they're feeling.

Even in nations one needs to ask what and how they feel on a given issue or subject before decisions are made, listening is important, you may be shocked they may aggress.

Reach out your hand and touché another heart, it very possible to gain a friend not just an acquaintance. Respect all nations as part of the whole, not living in ones personality which limit you, become one with all life.

"Let There Be Infinite Love for All Nations"

SUPERFICIAL CONCEPTS

People push away the truth and accept illusions. And they don't want you to show them the many things that need to be corrected or change in their society or individual lives. A good example is addicts, ones who are self-motivated by the stimulation of the substances that give them short-term pleasure, for instance the smoker whether drugs or cigarettes or whatever the substance it destructs their physical bodies. They have accepted the results as a part of their self indulge harm. They know the harm of these things, but they will not stop using them.

It's almost impossible to understand the reasoning these individuals have in regards to their life. I guess you are saying' she don't know how that person feel, it can be all they have in comfort." You are right I do not know this I do know if one must care about oneself to the point that nothing is as important as ones life.

It's like an external authority exist and the addicts are led to the lake to drown, they know they will die; it's just a matter of time. If they continuously use these substances life climax will end for them.

The mind is like the surface of a pond only rippled by the wind, when the wind moves over the surface a wave breaks and brings a state of movement and when the wind stop it returns to it rest. We are controlled by our own mentality if the waters are distorted as the wind of desires moves with its rippling waves to clouds ones reflection it becomes meaningless and of no value, with this shifting waves the control is in the wind to shapes ones destiny.

Humankind permits the winds of life disturbing events and difficulties to control. There is only one cause in each individual's life and that is one's own conscious creation, if the consciousness is focus on the superficial concepts, then the mind brings value to those things which are superficial, knowing only meaningful things can bring meaningful results, with the lack of concern for oneself the results become harmful.

Many yields to the images which are basically irrational and opposite to the truth, whether innocently or knowingly, they accept the responsibility to act and think with integrate consistency, and they support it by producing competitive values for others in loyalty to honesty, many are honest people, but they are blinded by illusions from others.

The deepest programmed behavior is in those who are looking for leaders, they have the concept that they are unable to make the right decision for themselves, or they are the mental lazy ones. Yes there are ones who can direct you to the right path, but once on the path it's up to you to function on that path for your success. No one should push or pull you along the way. Sometimes it may be difficult, to let your mind break free of its many imagines limitations.

All consciousness is separated, by one's own little hidden door in the innermost secret of one's soul, can open to the Cosmic Light, no matter how high or low ones level of growth towards the divine substance, we are united in the purpose. We have dreams and visions of God, God being an aspect of ourselves just as we dream in the image. All of the concepts of heavens and hells are within us although we make our own here on earth and all the creative thoughts are there to of the concepts.

The wonderful thing about mankind, we are highly intellectual minds with four function and a fifth one call the transcendent function, the one that helps one to attack the thought and carry it. There are sensation, thinking, feeling, and intuition, this function enables us to estimate the possibilities of a given situation, and these are the inward guides to what ones values are interrupted. In avoiding the stress of reprogramming your mind one must seek the path of least resistance as long as it's a positive one.

Being the children of the Divine, we are responsible for our inner and outer transformation bringing together the natural ingredient needed for transforming from the superficial concepts to reflect upon the experiments conducted on the higher plane of our spiritual nature and interconnection of the components of the universal expression.

It has long been known the development of people and civilization is influenced by the great rhythms of the earth and the celestial bodies, then why not respect the protective forces, and realize what is important, and that's being conscious of our true self and the purpose of the activity of this universe, and put away superficial concepts of life, It's time for all of mankind to focus, their energies to know of the mysteries of life.

Our minds and spirits are the keys to opening the unconscious trances. Questions, like can a man sin alone, are we all responsible for each other, are we being swept away by wrong judgments, are we influence by our emotions or by the motions of others, or are we guiltless in the crimes against humanity?

What of our root nature, is it spirit with mind that shapes our expressions through our individuality or are we just endowed with free will?

The very core of our nature, there is an activation of right and responsibility to choose. The difficulty arises from outside forces, others with their emotional will, which is stored up in the mind to influence one human being then another. We exercise one upon another.

We are connected, it's impossible to think if ones associations will not influence you, a dirty and foul person, their dirtiness will rub off on you, think about it, if as a dirty body is bathed in clean water, the water becomes dirty and foul after bathing. It's really, when you accept the dirt it's impossible not to pollute what's in the atmosphere around you, you are influencing others as well with the dirt you have encounter.

It does not have to be this way; we have the capacity to create and the freedom to choose. We see everyday people losing their true identities in the false superficial concepts, roles players unaware of the consequences. This is one of the great challenges in life for an individual to be just an individual not be in a co-depended situation, being at the call of another person's will for you, being a group thinker and actor, losing one's individuality.

The process of being an individual is a must not, saying you cannot aggress on a given subject with others, but still be in control of self. To become an ideal person, one who is on the upward arc, one that is self-conscious and evolving it takes concern and a feeling for the unknown to unfold.

Being superficial is our downfall, is slows the process of growth towards the ideal person, understand the purpose of growth is to expand up to join the Christ-Consciousness or Source (God-mind), which graduates us from beyond the human state, this will foreclose some unimportant things and place the person on the path or stage of growth with the ability to claim that special role of the spiritual human.

In order to allow the development of our individuality, The Source of Life (God) created us in immature form and gave us free choice, leaving space for us to grow, spiritually into unique, adult companions. Although some people take most experiences lightly and rebel to learning the basis, closing their minds from learning from those experiences, it will not close the door entirely to growth but it prolong the process of one growth by ones choices in one's life. We are given the opportunity to make right choices and wrong ones; we reap the results of those choices.

We learn through direct individual experiences that our choices whether constructive or destructive in thought, words, and deeds, which lead to greater harmony and peace or disharmony and distress in our lives as individuals and all who come in contact with us personally.

There are laws, which govern the universe, and we are subject to those laws, as well as all other entities in this universe, we will bring in our own reality into production by our deeds. If the individual thought patterns is dealing in turmoil the law of cause and effect tell us that nothing happen that is not of our own choosing even in ones associated environment one encounters, creates our own reality.

Its been said that we chosen all what happens to us and we grow through every experience life brings our way, but what of the associated world, other we do not have control that cause a person harm, one who is in the wrong place at the wrong time, is it fate or is it destiny for ones requirement to experience the mishap or not?

If a person makes a decision to be at a place at a given time one choose to be there, not saying it could be avoided, sometimes people do not listen to that inner voice that speaks to them to warning them of trouble, so is must be for a purpose. Understand our mental body is created to be a magnetic field through which the power of our attention is drawn to our presence protective forces into action. Most people do not voluntarily chosen to become in tune to the forces of God's Protective forces.

Sometime you wonder if you would be understood by others or even yourself at times, because of some of the choices you make.

Turning your attention for a moment to when you had opportunities to success in a journey that would have brought you to a place of harmony and peace but you choose to go in the other direction for whatever reason you do not understand?

We know, for whatever reason one makes wrong decisions there is a reason and perhaps we sometime do not reason out the situation first, it's not conscious in one's mind. It could be ones programming the unconscious, where one is programmed in the past, to be unconcern about oneself, meaning doing right for others and not for oneself.

One must exert his or her consciousness constantly, honestly in lifelong effort to maintain a prosperous, happy and healthy life style. There are people who have been programmed to self-sacrifice, even if there are no particular persons involved in the sacrifice, and there are those who are programmed for self-destruction.

Nevertheless we experience the driving force within our minds to choice which avenue in life we want our destiny to unfold. Whatever reason rather than rationalize our experiences in life and or its sorrows, our experiences are unfolding and it's difficult to get a clear sense of what one's next state or plan will be like.

The unanswered questions are still facing us why are we so superficial? Who are we only, seeing the outward state or surface meaning of things, and not seeing the deep profound things, and their mysteries, we must reach deep within and not limit ourselves in thinking about the true realities; although we cannot fool ourselves into thinking we can solve all life's mysteries. We can interact with the Source of all for the answers to what is comprehensive to our brain capacity.

In the meantime, we must not waste time with superficial concepts about life, or waiting on the sidelines merely an observer, keeping one eye open and the other close to what's happening around us over looking to most obvious.

No further explain to the respond of a superficial individual its only shows the vital touch of the indwelling to awake the true reality of it all.

"Draw On the Strength of What Is Real"

DELUSIONS OF THE TIMES

A person's consciousness is comprised of that of which he/she is aware or has been acquainted with through the experiences of their lives. The outer world of influences has divided the consciousness of the people by the spirit of the times which freedom of thoughts, actions and immoral believes are accepted as truth. Most developed nations are cultivating their people in the refinement in general education in the Arts, Tech., and Sciences, but deluding in the moral and virtues situations. These nations are taken grant steps backward in the moral issues being influence by the lesser refine or undeveloped ones in social refinements skills and the people are returning to the stone ages, Hair and Faces are not groomed, people are looking like cave-dweller.

It's the spirit of the times, where people are not caring about anything, even their language is misunderstood, tell me what is "dogs" people are not dogs, making their own language, that they who have the same mentality to understand. If you really look at the language it's like the cave dwellers, in the stone ages they made noises not speech and hand movements to communicate with each other. Tell me why are the societies of the world are moving backward? Can it be the overwhelming influences of different cultural backgrounds in the world today or it is people want to identify with different groups because of the lack of self-worth in whom and what you as an individual are? It's something to think about, moving right along.

More experiences in life come from the promotion of thoughts and ideas, which are brought into manifestation by ones activities. In today's world both men and women are focusing on achievements of some kind. The understanding if one has the knowledge and the tools, why not use them.

What is your specialty? Is it medicine, engineering, or the sciences, all such pride professions have their drawbacks; they are mostly depend on funds or approval from the nation's governmental machinery.

Even with the tools to become what you want, you may need to let go of certain attitudes or images before you can achieve your goals. Situations may hold you back, the challenges in society are broadcasting to you certain methods to use but they are not working what are you to do?

One must use one's ability and willingness to make moral judgments; it's a necessity to make sound decisions for any journey to be achieved. You may be thinking why must I make moral decisions? To answer that question understands the very foundation in any civilize society is based on morals and virtues.

In a society of reason and judgment ones values produce the outcome of whatever activity is created. Yet it is obvious that people are not using right judgment in the simplest decision-making. Many may argue with me on this, but the proof is in the pudding.

Whatever is happening in our lives is coming from an image one holds about a given situation or of oneself. If you are going back and forth doing the same things over and over with no change, there can't be a change. Each moment in time brings you closer to release issues or bind situations. If you expect answers to the conditions in your life to change for the better one must stop creating false illusions and using dishonest methods in ones activities.

Okay, you may say, I am doing all the right things and still I am not achieving my goals. I believe I am using the right judgment I am morally fair in my actions, so what's holding me back?

Who and what you are, have you ever thought about it really, or analysis the reasons for the issues, and conditions or the quality of your lives?

If you cannot see the reason why, than its time to go back into your memories and bring back the unconscious memories to consciousness, check the image you have of yourself, recall all the times you did understand events as they were happening. Then picture in your mind the images existed of that given situation, do you understand each contact with others and their views about a given issue or suggestion if accepted affects your life and did they limit or increase your chances for success?

Now there are other factor that we cannot overlook, the laws that govern life and nature. Our past incarnates, wrongs to put- right, lesson to learn, and the evolution of our consciousness to perfection in what we call the Christ-Consciousness, are in play.

Humankind exists and all nature in it defect forms exists and they both have the ability to develop in reasons of how and why things are as they are. We are both seeds that are cultivated in the beginning to expand to maturity. It's been said that animals consciousness cannot shift It's only from sensation of the outer world to the inner states of being, also they are unable to know itself, I wonder about that? Yes we know we humans have the ability to grow in ones mental consciousness The entire future of each individual is based on what is concealed in the individual creative ability to expand in consciousness, to know what kind of seeds gather to itself, being determine to grow with the recognition of all activities are guided by one's own intelligence, Mind, purpose, intuitiveness and desire, and if a person can admit and accept this beginning assured the results will be performed.

There are many feeling pressured, scattered unable to handle so many conditions they face each and every day, they dropout of society, turn to the acts of crime and violence, in results of their actions causing others to be subject to difficulties, confusion and hopelessness.

There are people who are acting surreptitiously, hush-hush, in any case their crimes is inflicted on the innocents as intended by the criminal minded underhanded not facing the individuals upfront, but working behind the hidden veil of untruths, in that dark secret places, where the moral responsibility lies, which has large impact on the entire society. The groups we respect, the professionals, the ones who are experts, ones schooled in their occupation of higher learning, the so-call masters. Some may say, your oppressor has nothing more than the power you confer upon him to destroy you. But one could understand the trust system; most people are focus on what is good about people then what they need to be aware of.

By nature, meaning ones true nature the Divine part that is still in each and every individual, even the wrong acting individual has some good, but it's so deep that it's hard to activate, because many have forbidden themselves to be a part of the true nature. In reality we all are a part of the Divine nature of our Creator (God).

Deception harms every value system; it touches honesty and every demonstration of love we have for each other. Some of the professionals avoid being honest to gain a profit; living by faking to extract power from others by their lack of knowledge of the situation at hand. First they undermine the concepts of values, and promote the false behavior between individual's offers the greatest capacity for love of one's fellowman.

Achievement in whatever- profession can not be totally experience or rewarding until a complete achievement in humanities, can ones life complete ones being, knowing professional do not make you trustworthy. Total well being only comes through honesty and development of values for ones self and society, by being an example.

For instance a doctor must feel somewhat impersonal in some cases otherwise his heart will be filled with pain for some he/she are unable to help, or those individuals beyond the call of ones understanding to perform to get a good result. But there are those who yield to the greed desire, ones who only see dollars signs, some patients are over medicated, some are subjected to unneeded surgery, why because there is more money in managing a condition then prevention. Mostly it's the HMO have a bases interest in prevention because their money comes in each and every month like clockwork if one is sick or not, where as others physicians need to see their patients to make money.

The prescription drug industry is making a killing by the recommendations of their drugs to the physician patients when they visit their offices. Do not think the doctors are not being rewarded from these companies; understand there is some not receiving. It is unavoidable in a sense we depend on the doctors for our physical health survival. This is a double burden on the patient we are trap in a system where the increasing power of one's life is being taken out of the individuals hand by those who want to exploit them. Then there are the ones who said they would help humanity for good without a clue.

Now let's look at others who are professionals in their fields, the engineers and builders, ones who construct our highways, bridges, and build our homes and office building, stores and eateries. The engineer designs a bridge or highway using specialized requirement for the builder to use, now let say, the builder use poor quality materials to cut-cost without the knowledge in the areas that the engineer may overlook upon inspection and let's say he gets by. But one or two years later an accident occurs, the investigation reveals the materials were below standards. In the long run the engineer is holding the bag.

Let's say you solicited a building contractor to build your dream home or a store whatever the contractor plans the work; you are vulnerable without knowledge of the process of the work.

I've addressed these examples to get your attraction to establish a need to know something about every situation or project before journeying in. Teach your children at a very early age just maybe they will have a more successful life than normal.

Very often we find ourselves involved in situations with others, whom we may not know personally, but the situation calls for interaction, for whatever reason we become connected. We affect each other where to built –up or take-down a change takes place, we touch from within and without creating a new foundation which built and or lessons are learn, and all of these things unfold to offer guidance, support or enlightenment for our path in life.

Have you ever wondered why people hide their true feeling? We all are guilty of that try of activity from time to time for whatever the reasons it verse from a situation and or events. If you really want to know of anything in life, and the reasons why we act as we do use yourself for an example by sitting down focusing your mind on nothing else except the situation or event at-hand, remove all the other issues that come to mind.

As the unconscious brings to conscious from within your memory see yourself and see the image of yourself begin to unfold. If you find yourself questioning what you see, take a few minutes, think of peacefulness in your mind, and ask for clarity and truth and let it come willingly known as truth flows to you.

Each moment has its highest purpose we touch each other for that higher purpose as we focus on the good about that person to enable us to achieve a good relationship although one must be watchful of the ones you meet. Watch because all people are not trustworthy watch their words, sense their energy and see if there is more here than meets the eye. Above all be true to yourself, you have two choices perfect you're higher self or relax in the narrow lost vision for the future.

Let's move to another area to think on, it's been expressed that mankind has only been civilized for a few thousand years. If you really believe that, although it's been discovery and proven differently mankind has excised long beyond the written record. Now if you regard civilized as being a group of people appears and give the impression to be refine, socially organized, or educated in showing others consideration.

Its how you look at civilization and what is meant by civilized?

Think about it, mankind is a conscious being, and as we know they have been ones with consciousness since the separation of sexes. There is a spiritual cord, which emanates from the Divine center of our being that set us apart from the other kingdoms as spiritual-consciousness is concern. We as humans have three major divisions in our aspects of being, which work together representing the trinity aspects of creation in mankind. What we call the waking conscious mind, the subconscious mind, and the super conscious mind; it's the consciousness cord-extending link between them.

This is another story entirely concerning mankind ability to be civilized. Think on the aspects of the so-call tree of life and the tree of the knowledge of good and evil in mankind so speculated. The aspects of man are which makes man a trinity, are spirit, soul and personality. The Spirit is the Infinite Energy of the highest planes beyond the relative understanding, it serves all of existence and we have a part of that existence within us, allowing us to share in the source of love and wisdom; think about this, as you consider the lines, Edwin Arnold in a poem! "Never the Spirit was born; the spirit shall cease to be never!

45

Birth less and deathless and changeless remained the Spirit forever; death hath not touched it at all, dead though the house of it seems." If you can grasp the true meaning to the statement, then you are opening to yourself realization.

If one is confuse in part, I will give you something to think about to come possible clear.

When one looks at living beings and or life creatures what do you see? A form of life in some material body, It is a live functioning in its own form, but alive and that life substance has no beginning or ending, so what is it? Soul is not only the intermediate

Aspect of life to animate the essence of the physical body in the individual personality, it's the substance that evolves or disgust, it has the lower concrete mind, the mental body the mind stuff, and the higher spiritual or abstract mind. These aspects of the soul are qualities bring into being to the human kingdom and enable mankind to contact both the lower kingdoms in nature and the higher spiritual realities.

Most people think the soul is perfect, that's because ones spiritual eye has not opened to the point that its reality has been reviewed into its oneness of the inner-knowing. Think if the soul was perfect, would persons be doing evil in their lives? The soul is where the site of consciousness and one knows the person's consciousness governs one's thoughts and actions.

Let's think on one of the stories in regard to the creation of humankind, the story go like this "God made man from the dust of the earth and breath in his nose the breath of life and he became a living soul, and as he progressed to a place of being conscious of him- self and his actions." Can you see why the soul must elevate, to assist the other aspects of their individual form toward perfection?

As for the body it's a form of matter, which we use to live our life's quest. As we all know that matter changes in the process of the change, it take on different forms and once it decays and lose its ability to function for its purpose in this crest it goes back or change for other uses.

People are beginning to see the unreality of the material things around them great as these material things may seem to be, it's not enough to have material things for they are here today and gone tomorrow. Someone said; "do not lay up things where the theft can steal. But place your hopes and dreams on things eternal," meaning your Divine Source which gives you life everlasting.

Since humankind has been given the choices in life by ones creator, response to that freedom and being an infancy without a clue produced one's own creations, through the pathway of expression and the emotional energies experience by the individual, have develop one's own personality. With this own conscious humankind has extended ones building a veil mentality between ones upper and lower personality in mind, caused many to product weaknesses because of self -defeated in mind.

The delusions of the times, at the present stage in mankind's history, mean there must be a releasing of purified, powerfully discharge of personal encouragement of life, and make it accessible to those seeking spiritual truth, and those who cannot solved their own mystery in life, with civilized love and call to divine energy to animate the impulse of mankind hearts to be directed by their higher mind. Nullifying the past non-constructive effects will change the record of mankind individually in the present of their bad karma.

The time will come when all humankind will be ultimately dissipated all the bad karma and the record will be clean and civilize people can be civilize to one another and the plan will be completed for humankind.

Human's s is destined to be whole and divine; we must depict the complete plan for humankind as a whole. We cannot place a square in a round hole and fill all the space within the circle, but with divinity that shows light, light will fill all the space within a circle. It's all about aligning oneself with the divine purpose for mankind. One must touch upon the things of spirituality in order to stimulate ones awareness of the divinity. Forget the outer appearance of the spirit of the times and focus on changing the times toward your highest spiritual potential.

You may be thinking, "How and why shall I work towards my destiny"? Is it for me to know or can I change it, what do I need to do? These are questions that perhaps interring your minds. First most people question how can we know what our destiny is, and what is desired by our Creator? First one must fine the general overall ideal person (example) to be like, and work from there. Second we know the prefect -will is where we must be in order to please our Creator. Third we must seek perfection and purity of heart and mind to reach a higher level of evolutional progress.

The quality of every moment effects the present and future in each of our lives, not only for us as individual, but others as well, those who touch our lives by association or otherwise. If we think a thing through before acting we will have fewer difficulties in everyday life.

The delusion of the times are related to what is hidden in the minds of many less evolved individuals, and the wise ones are not exercising their knowledge to assist the expanding of the ones less knowledgeable about the Laws which govern the universe.

The delusions of the times are demonstrated in the form of emotionalism, whether conscious or unconscious the activities correspond to the physical body and carnal experience. All represents what happen when the emotional side is allowed to control and run wild to overcome ones rational and reasonable mind. Moreover it demonstrates the emotional side will occasionally lead to circumstances in which the thought processes will be controlled by their unproductive emotions.

Being under the powerful influence of emotionalism, the seed of many struggles have occurred and form a deliberated structure for permanent damage to society. When there is hate, overly sexual free and deception taught to the young society it's held there in the heart to remain and acted on and transferred to the new generation.

And those that initially created the spirit of the times for profit or just to be able to feel they are in control of their desires in the form of emotionalism has passed through the gateway of death and lift their distorted impact on the present generation to overcome.

We have identified the great temptations of the times, and we see the flood- gates are open and the force of it is very strong and the destruction is great. The underlying spirit of truths is still available to humankind, if they are willing to open their eyes and hearts to them.

A point must be stressed, the emotional cord which records all your emotional lives and its weaknesses, and if one is to gain strength from all ones incarnated lives one must evolve each life-time to a higher level. The emotional seed atom registers the emotional qualities of an individual desires whether good or bad.

We know in the case of death, the basic qualities of a person character cannot change being dead physical is only the anatomy, not the evolving soul. One is still left with all their weaknesses and strengths to carry over to the next lifetime. The difficult in accepting that more error in judgment brought on by ones emotional outbound caused by unconscious accounts and all the past is in a real sense present now.

Some of you may be thinking if what I've said it true the past is going to come back in the next life in form of bad karma, we do not have a chance. First one must understand that karma is not a form of punishment; it's a gift to you gives the opportunity for you to change your character.

One doesn't need to follow the cultures of the time, but advance your minds to reach the structures of underline laws of nature and God. Remember no one deserves to have a non-productive attachment, lifetime after lifetime because of following the spirit of the times.

The most important thing to remember is emotionalism needs not to decide whether or not a particular act is worthy of your attention. The law of nature and of God governs every effort and aspects of mankind's existence on every level of thought, emotion and ones expressions. The purpose of opening one's eyes is to see the need for change, God lays it all out before you as an intend to assist you to reach higher realms in ones consciousness, the achievement of essential principles that seem to be lost, in this delusion of the times.

No doubt at some point in reading this view not allowing fear to restrict ones process a clarity came to your minds about all the events you have experience could have been avoided if you had taken the time to think things through before acting.

It's the hardest thing to break free of the things you have learn over time, one becomes afraid to dance to a new tune, a new way of living to reach ones goals in life. You may have experience the emotion of fear, yes it's an emotion to fear, all emotions are not unproductive only the ones that cause you grief, all emotions penetrates, the necessary and the unnecessary ones, no matter what type of emotions one have only the one that bring sorrow are the ones to discard from your character.

There are good rewarding areas one can receive in the form of emotions, Love, compassion, devotion and forgiveness etc.; Theses are true form of the positive emotions that brings on a good change in society.

If we are to see a positive change in society we must change the flow of the non-productive impact of the spirit of the times.

Open your hearts and mind release the positive energy around you into the atmosphere of earth to all inherits to receive your new found clarity, and be an illuminable light to manifest all right activity of one's emotionalism, in the present delusional times.

Innocent World

People even in these day and times are blind to life's stages and the minds at work. Even the older ones are so very innocent of the world in which we live in. Maybe I should say, societies, in which we live our societies, groups, families, government, religions etc., so many are so trusting to other people, and so many are using deception and other forms of evil-means to enslave others minds and means.

Some people prefer to be tied down, bound into one way of thinking, comfortable in the answers that someone else provides, not knowing deception it in play, but willing to accept through their innocents in their world.

Being innocent dose not exempt you from the system experiences, there is no reason for you to not seek-knowledge before-hand in any decision making which could cause large problems later in one's life, examine your own motives and integrity and see what chains are imposed upon it. It is time to become aware of what others are doing to you by way of sweet words and repetition advertisement to promote their ideas and desires on you. Understand everything comes with a price, and you may not want to pay. Being innocent in mind dose not remove you from responsibility of your decisions.

Being innocent of the knowledge of how the governments or religions, social groups or even ones families members use suggestions that dominate you and chain you, you are in a system of slavery a delusional world. A situation where either reward or punishment, acceptance, security is use to deceive or manipulate another it's an artificial society.

Examine your own feeling about society and the world as a whole. Do not take anything at face-value. You are the only ruler and controller of your own mind and body. By being the ruler one must understand the need for balance, and a good ruler develops virtues and personal power to ever situation.

In order to understand any situation in one's life one should ask question first of oneself to help to become aware of one's problems and achievements. Knowing much of our programming is by society, it shapes our world views; it is the common values, ideas, mores, and taboos, which shape our world.

Humankind habitual reinforce these patterns society layout for its people, without thought of the results, of those decisions. Perhaps a change in one's own behavior is in order?

Sometimes people are trap in problems and have excuses for their situation because of what has been programmed in their minds by their society.

It may be time to clear the mind, do some mental house-cleaning and by examining one's own society. Why I say this is because people jury other countries, and not seeing their own.

Clean your own house first one needs to go within oneself push-out all outer social suggestions that are not constructive and for your good.

Perhaps an examination of what's good means, one can be locked into habitual behavior that may or may not be for ones good and it is because a shield is in place to keep out the good and one from seeing the truth of one's wants for one's life.

If one start to look within one-self deeply closing off from the outside world for a short time the answers will come from within the inner-part of you that great-powerful energy that governs all life, holes the keys to all answers in the universe.

And So Will Be the Change

*"The delusions of the Now Will Not All ways be
in Control of the World or it's People"*

THE UNFOLDING OF HUMAN CONSCIOUSNESS

The entire thought system and activities of humankind is based on the state of the individual conscious development or evolvement, you may say ones growth is in one's ability to reason or ones cultural refinement.

When the real knowledge of one's nature becomes manifested in its qualities, the real self takes control. The Divine spark no longer is hidden in the lower part of mankind consciousness... In reality when the real self begin to unfold, you become conscious of not only the outer world you also become self-conscious, letting the real self free to awaken, and set aside from ones lower self and all the things which causes bondage.

Understand, although we are imperfect in many things, it's important to take a few moments each day to go within to garner the inward powers of our mental senses to direct and guide us. Before mankind became evolved to be able to reason there was a master controller, after the time of receiving consciousness the controller who gave us the control of ourselves, trusted us to do at will, but it came with a price we tried but lost control of ourselves and caused chaos in our own lives.

Until we as humans awake and unfold into the knowledge of nature, and examine into what is real and having regard for others purpose in life, knowing we all perform differently in the stages of our own experiences. Then we will have arouse out of sleep, and see or respect the world around us, knowing the world will not vanish if we are not here, and be willing to accept life as being good, and recognize it as the manifestation of the Divine intention. Not as the distortion of a dream world of hatred and destructive events that many humans are trying to induce.

First one must understand, we are the product of one's social environment, although the economic conditions play a part in situations, as our consciousness unfold one will realize we are living beings with need for eternal existence, and no moment in this life or other lifetimes will there be without a record of one's events or activities from the time of one's creative origin, so we are accountable for all our activities. When, you become conscious of this fact and bring the concept into the realm of your actual consciousness the enfoldment will take place in one as an individually.

"By their fruits shall you know them," is it safe to say this rule applies to all life? We judge, everything by its quality, it matters not if its fruits are meals, entertainment, and works etc., results of good quality is the only things one is willing to accept.

We wish to stiffen the fact you are real beings made from the Absolute Source, but little below the lower gods, but all are manifestation of gods. Who is the Absolute? Understand, we are products of the god's goodness and perfection, and our mission is to unfold these qualities, which are ones inheritances from the relative Source-God.

In Accepting ones inheritance, and assert ones divinity, one will step onto the pathway, which unfolds ones true-consciousness.

When we realize we are only a part of own Universe, which is foundered on a great life principle in which is unchangeable and everything is related to each other and this universe is one- part of the great emanation of the Absolute. And the merging of self into one great self to suppose the extension of all the individuals consciousness responds, and until taken in the whole picture, which appears to be mysterious to many now.

The mysteriousness of our being is not confined to subtle physiological processes, which we have in common with all animal life on this planet. There are higher and more captivating powers in our human personality, which many are refusing to express. The great depth of our very existence is the hidden life that dwells in the spirit of the

Gods mysterious complexity of our personality affirms that Humankind will fine its way to the truth about self and ones very existence in time.

The mind as it reaches for the consciousness by inspiration of the Godhead, instinctively desires the spiritual revelations of truth of its origin. One must understand mind and consciousness are different, as for consciousness it's the primal, nebulous, the invisible energy comprising of all of totality, consciousness and life is said to be identical, and it doesn't take up space, my thoughts are based ones inner belief which gives one a feeling of awareness or awakens to the reality of a given thing. Annie Besant says consciousness is an attribute or characteristic; knowing that we know, many different in their view in consciousness take Carl Jung says, consciousness arises from the psychotic of personality, depending upon the patterns of behavior and the psychic contents that are primarily unconscious. Definitions are constantly changing do to the evolution of consciousness.

The mind has the attendance to shift gradual or suddenly done to changing in one's life-style and attitudes to emotions traumatic, restlessness etc., if one think along the parapsychology lines than one must look beyond the view of the physical brain, one of the expansion of mind and an ethereal vibration frequency that contains an individual's Akashi Records and their present belief system, which subconscious mind, bio-computer and ones soul mind.

There is what we call mind-energy which originates from Cosmic Energy and it enters the head constantly in minutes quantities to reach the pineal gland where it is transmuted into electrical energy to be used by the brain area, then travels to the pituitary gland where it is transmuted into physical energy suitable for use by the glands and the physical body systems.

Enough of the consciousness and mind, at these time, later more on the subject let's move on to another area briefly touch on the psychological cause of diseases in the nature of one's emotional system.

First, it needs to be said; the true cause lies hidden in the past of the planetary life, and generally the premise is beyond our power to grasp and to express for our mental ability is inadequate for the task. It's better for us to admit that it is impossible for Humankind to understand the mystery or the deep-seated causes for the emerging of the different problems which off-set Humankind in the form of diseases in their lives, basically disease it shown in all form in all the life entities. That means the ultimate cause lies beyond our comprehension, and the intent as it is lies hidden in the mind of the source of disease.

What do we really know about diseases? The best minds only see partly and can only deal with the surface causes. So we are going to touch a few of those general causes, where our intelligent can understand. All disease comes from the lack of harmony in body, mind and spirit. The lack of harmony produces the ideal condition for all forms of diseases not only physically, but mentally as well.

All disease is caused by disharmony in some form or another, the lack of alignment and control of one's true nature.

It's been said that wrong human thoughts will not cause diseases, well I differ in my view, understanding that the law of cause and effect governs disease as well as all other activities of creation in which all the kingdoms convey.

Let's look at disease as a fact in nature, it's found in all four kingdoms in Nature.

Disease is like a seed planted in the earth that for whatever reason grows to destroy the earth, which houses it. We have tendency to focus our attention on the unnecessary operations of everyday life, which performs below or above the field of consciousness and not of the rational processes of the mind.

The average person recognizes their strong and weak points in their own character, but fails to recognize the unconscious modification of their character each day by ones associations certain things which may have caused an unwanted change or a non-productive form of emotionalism which, in results develops a disease.

Reason being, each person has their own energy and the energy function is what makes the body automate which gives one the inner strength. Ones stream of life, anchored in the heart, determines the vitality of the person, so if an undesired change takes place the body becomes out of order. One becomes captive in ones very existence and the control of one's expression falls upon the physical plane open to the weakest placed upon it.

Because of the three types of energy used in the expression of mankind, as being the energy of life, non-productive energy of one's personality and last but not least the positive energy of one's soul. As mankind being created as a Trinity expression, the three aspects are developed individually according to the evolvement of the individual. If the individual energy is disturbers, likewise man's body manifest intertwines of the other energy arising in the emotional and mental bodies.

Majority of human beings are influence by their associative environment and impulses relating to one's own basic conditions, the impulses coming from the mental plane. When the individual is being imposed upon by an unavoidable situation the body reacts in different ways of expresses, at time it causes disease.

The human body have its focusing point for ones interior energy and that energy may not be ones vital energy being used, understand the qualification of force comes from ones emotional apparatus accordance to ones personality development. The basic energy pouring into the body conditions the physical body.

Let's explain energy more define but briefly, there are two major types; the ray energy of the soul and the ray energy of the personality, qualified by the three minor rays which is also forces, the rays of one's mental nature, the astral body, and ones physical vehicle, therefore it involves five energies that are present in the ether body.

Maybe a brief explanation of ether body is in order, the ether body is ones mechanism of vital panic life or underlies the outer familiar equipment of the nervous system, which feeds and actuates all parts of the physical organism.

The main causes of all diseases are two nature, the over stimulation or no stimulation of the centers. We as humans are very emotional and quick to act in all the events in our lives, we are impulsive in our activities, physically and mentally, this can cause over active or the under active of any center in any part of our body. Where there is correction of the flow of energy in commensurate to the desires or demands of our physical body at any particular stage of one's development, there is a chance for freedom from disease.

Moving right along, we are complicated entities and we must constantly adapt to situations and conditions of our associations and environment, remembering the god-spark of divinity originated in our universe, which certainly is unfolding our intelligent and directing our course in life.

Every round has its special lesson to awaken humanity, thus we see how immature and inhumane man is yet act like a mere child crying out for things they cannot understand, many when reach an age of maturity are seeking materialists and power which they cannot control, believing it will complete ones purpose, without a clue of their own real nature for millions of years continuously going in circles. So many not realizing their true purpose or their relation to others they war with, and as they destroy ones fellowmen, parts of their selves are being destroyed too.

Every individual has a lower consciousness (instinctive) mental region within them and from it are constantly arising impulses and desires that are to perplex and annoy, but it's the lower form of the human life. It's their lower consciousness, by using instinct only one is like the lower animal, but there are some animals have developed the ability like rudimentary intellect or reason, which enables them to meet new conditions. The point is whether mankind will master their lower selves?

Reaching back through history of humans, the caveman to the technical and science discovery age, we see little progress in the evolvement of consciousness in the form of humanness toward one another, we still fight each other for whatever reason at times we do not know the reason just the idea to destroy someone or something for no real purpose. We see no change from the generations of our ancestors still constantly permitting impulses to rule one's life.

Unguarded animal instincts, passions, appetites, desires, feelings, sensations, emotions, etc., are the factors in the whole situation of mankind state, it kills the desire of life. One must eradicate the old way from the mind, idea that physical life is everything and one must recognize the fullness in life is to expand the light within each of us.

I wish to explain, mankind has lived on the Earth for more than four million years, the first two golden ages were magnificent there was no imperfections, but as mankind began to claim the ability of self choice that was given to them by ones Creator God, turning their thoughts downward which shut the door to the luminous light of perfection.

The doors stands open at any time for one to come into perfection and that's a good thing, but one must release the old downward nature of imperfection that gives one limitations by activities of hatred, envy, jealousy, revenge, and gratification of one's sexual impulse etc., these are things which constantly intruding upon mankind attention slowing their progress in asset ones self-mastery.

Dear ones how can you be beautiful if your activities are full of Chaco and deception? It would be a wonderful thing if humankind awakes in consciousness to the point of loving rather than hating and never letting a thought or feeling pass through one's mind which has no value for the good of others as well as oneself.

We know the free will of humans may not be interfered with, because individuals must choose how they are going to life and use the gift of this mighty energy, which flows through their bodies from the presence of God, but be real only good can come from good activities.

One should let their true- expression, which is the divine part to impel one to do things right better than they have been done before, not saying that one could triumph over others, but because for mankind to improve things he must start with self for it to be done better.

The brute instincts are still with us from the golden ages, constantly forcing themselves into our streams of thought, if only we would listen and learn to curb and control ones lower-parts (instincts), and reach for the higher parts, focusing them to higher mental ideals which will unfold ones consciousness to the higher plane of the Spiritual Consciousness, that state of consciousness which is the great prize that awaiting those who put forth the effort to free the human race and oneself from the lower consciousness, and the reward is worthy of one's effort.

The most important thing in every one life is to be successful at whatever one's dose, although, we come into the world unprepared and without a clue for that success. We must have instruction and guidelines to follow. Unfortunately, the guidelines and instructions are not enough for a successful life.

If a person knew the truth about the natural laws, and the purpose of these lifetimes, one would be full of potential for a successful life.

When it comes down to it each person must be brought to the truth of one's own nature, many of us have lost the concepts of their Divine nature through varies means.

Think about it, from birth to adulthood, we develop mental character, which directs our lives. You would not think about a new born having character, we start developing mental character day one of our physical incarnation.

From the womb to the twelfth month of life the newborn learns semi-stability, through the feeling of emotion (physically) the touch and feeling of love from parents, and others who come in their space and contact. As they start learning their physical identity, all their acts are emotional, with the lack of disciple, they becomes restless, unknowing of damages and being undeveloped fears takes place.

In the overlapping of development at the age of six months to two years the child becomes very conscious of the emotional identity they have. They develop attachments, from eighteen months to four years. The ego identity steps in ones self-esteem, vitality, purpose, strength of one's wills by the time the human is four years old the development social identity comes in and they become self-accepted.

The human ability to reason causes one to stand firmly, it enables one to speak so that one's words will reach others, even when one is unconscious of the fact its possessed their view and understandings, it rewards or damages the progressive and or enfoldment of oneself or others character starts to form.

First one must understand even though the present social and environmental influences, contribute to our character building, in this stage of time, we must not forget also our past lives come into play.

We are what we are not only from present situations, but past as well simply because in our past lives we have done, or left undone, certain things that needs closer.

It does not mean we are being punished, or no form part of the law all the time, if one is in a bad situation at the present time, it could be a desire one merely want to learn from. But understand if we manifested bad karma it will come up again in another lifetime if not reform or transform in this life before physical transition of this body, it will come up again as the results of one's own creation.

If you drive a car downs the wrong side of the street, look for a car coming to face you. That's the same as one desire to do something one know it's not accepted in the society one lives and try to get by, one has to nurse the condition created by ones desire which brought certain effects of more or less unpleasant and painful.

Moreover, once one has had one's eyes opened to the nature of their trouble and realize the fruit of their irresistible desire has greatly disappointed them, and it's time to become smart and let the pain fade away and move on to a brighter future in the present, hoping for a better life in the next one.

We all draw to us the things, which we expect, it's when we recognize our lives are not merely for our individuality, but we are needed to perform our individual contribution to society as a whole, assist mankind on an upward trend.

But no matter how important or less important one state in society there is something one can contribute to the betterment of the whole.

In the law of life no matter what ones present condition, if one belief system is strong enough ones faith will maintain or establish the change of the tide in the flow of events for the better.

Ones faith is one of the greatest assets to achievement and success in whatever undertaking and it's independent of all other beliefs or resolutions.

Faith gives an individual the reserve power of one's creator to be released in one's life, gives one the conviction, and courage to venture into the deep, practically the outstanding desires. The most important things in life are free; Love, Faith, will, and determination.

Let me point out a few; Love is the source of life, comes from our Creative Source (God). It's the natural law of life, which asks nothing of us, but to receive and give of its goodness. Love is the strongest law in existence. It's the center which all revolves around, it's the seat of the heart and mind attempt to superimpose itself upon what is said to be the greatest commandment in ones belief system. Above all it is the binding force and law in the universe and God is the authority and dictator of the gift of Love. As for Faith the attitude of an individual, above all determines how more effort is committed to ones belief of a given thing. It does not matter whether it large or small a belief is faith. It's a feeling deep within you saying is will manifest. Faith is being confident in knowing whatever will happen. Faith in something known deep within you, a knowing you will rise the next morning or not rise. Faith is beyond expectation of failure that God will not permit the sun to rise or the rain to fall. Faith is a deep knowing of all things work in divine order.

As for Will, it has to do with mental control, understand there is nothing permanent about ones will; it changes as a new desire comes to mind. If you want to think of will as a mental state as being a force of habit of thoughts persevere in attainment to one's own realization, for in the degree that you realize your dominance over your mind, so will be your control of it and its amenability to that control. So you see the true will brings realization of what the mental desire regards as a need to be or have the controlled will bring results for you.

Whatsoever is lodged within the heart and allow harvesting by one's mind effort are the results of determination. Think about it, if a lazy person who sleeps till noon cannot expect to get the harvest of a person who starts their day at day- break. There are many causes for success or failure, determination in whatever direction one desires, is the key.

In being determine in your efforts and putting the law of cause and effect in action, one becomes free from the bondage of that old ignorance of fear, believing that lie, you cannot succeed and have a successful life. The law of thought "As a man think so is he." The way one thinks determines how one's life will be. No one can govern your life but you no one else lives or share your body but you.

We as individuals determine the outcome of our own efforts, which brings the results in the issues and conditions of our lives. A sure way to fail in whatever it takes to be successful in life is to dwell on non-productive thoughts, and letting doubts lodge in your minds.

One must discovery the power within you and coupe it with good thoughts using right methods to achieve success, only with positive thoughts and efforts in showing determination.

All that you hope to be and move towards can be achieved if you have a positive mind, Will, Determination and Faith within self and you're Creator.

Ones happiness is in the hands of oneself. Stop poisoning your own mind with doubts and fears, most of all those things, which develop ones character and cause future self-punishment. Remember no one can live and have a joyful life without having a positive state of mind and maintain that positive attitude throughout the course of one's life.

Since we are focusing on the enfoldment of the human consciousness it's important to touch as many points as possible. The law of learning is a desire, one must want to learn, and even in children they start learning in the womb of its mother. The child learns first from parents, then family relations, environmental or nation, then the world etc., as they say, "no man is an island unto oneself." A large part of our learning comes from others, in form of observation, experiences and studies. By us being social creatures, and want approval and acceptant without waiting we act and react to others accordingly of the importance of the situation or condition.

The mysteriousness of our being is not confined to the subtle physiological processes, which we have in common with other creatures, but we are required to learn, not only social and complex personality of self and others to be able to commutates, one must link with one's own spirit matter and the deep-down hidden remarkable substance of ones being.

The mind is like a puzzle trying to place the pieces in their proper places. Humans learn by observation, we inherited the ability to question, which bridge mankind with the universe. Thoughts determine success or failure in one's life; we are the fruit of our own thoughts.

Every thought contributes to the future of our being, think about the days you may have an unkind thought, and how is made you feeling? That thought effect you more so then the situation or person you felt the thought for, you became disturbed or depressed.

Understand the consciousness is sending impels to the subconscious mind to store, to be a part of the collective unconsciousness, as we know life is formed from the inside out, and the stored thoughts emerges in other type of activity. Be it jealousies, friendship, love or hate, all of which oneself has dumped there. The way you think is the way you live.

Thought is an energy field of the cosmic awareness, it matters not if the thoughts are positive or non-productive they all create and are buried deep in ones subconscious mind and is used to intermesh with ones conscious mind, being placed into action for material appears.

As one moves toward the manifestation of the thought into being by repeating and applying more energy one begin to realize what a terrific force a thought has and it's unlimited in its creation.

I've been really inspired to write this part, what do you think of memory, do you really understand the important of keeping positive thoughts in your mind? There is a law to memory I will focus briefly on the subject because memory is an extensive subject.

One may say that the law of memory is the light on the pathway in developing ones plan for life. The mind is very similar to a phonograph, which records the deep impressions, understanding, awareness's, perception, associations, and visualization etc., before the eye can see with the clear vision one must be grown capable of the proper interpretation of what one see.

Memories can be valuable, in life we all need to remember things, which assist us in our survival, successes and mainly of our failures for improvements to enrich our lives.

The events and memories in history that has been written come to harvest its fury on this generation. The inhumane acts preformed by the earlier generations have allowed their moods and passion to rule and passed the same moods and passion to flow over into this generation with the same mind, to perform crimes of, murder, rape, and robbing etc.

The Nations around the world are in an all time high of evilness, the street, cities and towns are not safe from the beasties of man-kinds mind day or night. It's hard for anyone to believe that people are wondering why the chaos, sickness and diseases, when the seeming activities of so many are immoral. Massive disorder is in the land, people are perplexed, their minds are confused disconnected from their spiritual values, and declining in moral values as well.

The cause of it all people will not let go of the past influences of old habits and ideas. Growth will separates individuals from their old belief systems, which only harms and not heal. I will not go in detail of the obvious, it goes without saying it's all around you, the high tensions in mankind.

We shape our today and tomorrows by the mind-set we have today, reaching back to times of yesterday, as it brings certain results that we must endure. The law of cause and effect operates in our every thought and physical action, not only for individuals, but our whole world is affected.

There is another law, one of responsibility, we are responsible for our own actions, and we have no choice, only accept responsibility. People try to change the natural course of life, it will not work. The plan desired for a purpose of order to keep things in balance.

Humans need to cease blaming their problems on unseen forces accept the truth outside forces can only do what it permitted to happen. People seem to run away from responsibility, even the responsibility for one's own lives; they look at responsibility as a job. The more one's attention is focus on bitter experiences one will not be able to learn prevention.

Every day good or disrupt registers, in ones daily activities, it's our responsibility to use the best advantages our mental instruments, memory Noble people take personal responsibility in approaching the realms of peace, morals, honest and faith, cultivating their minds to be totally responsible all of their activities and thoughts.

Humans through centuries has qualified the universal substance with perish ability and limitation and use their bodies to express characterizes. The human race has storms of hate, anger, revenge, and, many other out-bursts of feelings of which has recorded those qualities to return them to us in form of attraction, the law of cause and effect.

The people of earth have cataclysm of thought and feeling as resentment against each other, sending out the feeling of revenge. All of these qualities are being recorded expresses of one's consciousness in which goes back to the source, the individual by means of chaos in the mind and in their lives.

Humanity must learn the law of the circle, the law of the One. Knowing the qualities generates and must receive it back into the minds and bodies of the individual, knowing the Universe and its substance move in circles and returns unto its source.

There is a self-generating and self-purifying force within nature and it's in each and everyone, which rises and throw-off all that disagrees with the law of the One who created "All." This force of energy is a pushing activity from within out and is the one power expanding our lives, but with free-will or choice in one's mind or consciousness to activate its power.

We must become channels for the positive aspects of life, directing our consciousness to concepts for only good to come to us. And if good is to come to us we are to generate that good to others as well. Our every space should be filled with love for ones fellowman, and creatures alike. We are not just physical matter, but divine energy in forms that mystery of life that we do not entirely understand.

Yes, there are concerns one must first want to know ones inner being or ones entire make-up, before one works toward the ultimate goal of come self-realized. Those who develop their inner powers and use the laws in place for us to follow will discover by surrendering to these laws. As one is awaken to these laws the real divinity of oneself is realized.

Let's talk about the unconscious and how it plays in our lives it's primarily one of the principle parts, which makes a human being an individual, which thinks and acts different from each other of who and what he is; it's this principle which forms the character unknowingly.

First a person looks into a mirror sees one's own face, but not really seeing the person hidden in the reflection of the mirror, ones shadow self that no one sees the unpleasant you, not even you see. In the realm of consciousness we are our own masters; we seem to be the factors themselves.

We seem to need to be convinced that the unconscious is regarded as a sort of in capsulated fragment of our most personal and intimate life.

As for collective unconsciousness it's a part of the psyche which can be the non-productive distinguished from ones personal unconsciousness by the fact that it does not owe its existence to one's personal experience, while the personal unconscious is made up of contents thoughts, which have at one time or another been conscious that has been repressed or forgotten, it's been said that unconscious consist of nothing but content accidentally deprived of consciousness or indistinguishable from the conscious materials, then as one's mind expand the will demand will enable the psyche to be identified in the individual.

It's back to what I've said first the unconscious is ones character unknown to oneself. In the first place, the mind when directed toward a certain thing a set of objects become very alert to discover things concerning those objects or ideas and the facts tend to seize whatever consciousness is willing to respond to its call.

I will be brief from this point on the subject of one's consciousness moving right along, when one begins to realize that we are capable of extending outwardly toward an object, material or mental and examining it by different methods inherent in itself, extracting knowledge regarding the object or by impresses perform mentally directed by ones sub-conscious mind to complete the task. What we extract is most wonderful and the process by which the knowledge comes is below the plane of consciousness, the work of the conscious mind being chiefly concerned in holding ones attention upon the object.

There is a law we haven't talked about, and that's' the law of learning. To be successful in life ones must be a student of life, everyone must decide whether one is going to be a success or a failure on this journey. If one refuses to be drawn into the path of learning that will raise one above the level of yesterdays weakens and past mistakes one is subject to repeat.

What I mean by repeat rebirth on the same level as before, no growth or elevation of one's consciousness or evolvement

If one comes back on the same level will it be painful or pleasure for the individual or will one suffer or be in despair? Understand there is no escape one must learn or repeat.

Learning is an opportunity and necessity it removes limitations and give ones awareness to overcome many kinds of challenges, and it also can be rewarding as well a painful. Sometimes, one chosen to wait too long to start action toward their goals and it become only a dream, never a reality.

It's been said the true teacher is life and we learn by trial and error, but remember life itself is given to us by choice and if one refuses to learn the basics requirements for living one is wasting time. I feel we are merely a pawn in a great game of chess, and being directed by some greater power as means for us to become the perfect image of goodness, and create some real changes in conditions in the world.

We should work on the reasons that mankind is full of shame, by the past and present world state of affairs, it can be rectify. By learning to change to do better we rid mankind of its shame, and this will change the future events.

The question we must look at, if each individual is willing to take a little time out each day to read something that would assist or inspire mankind in ones journey to perfection and act on it a change will occur.

All of us are uniting in this one thing, the journey of life; we are individuals in this quest, humans, animals, and vegetation, minerals all of us are in the same boat. But all of humanity as a whole must join together for the survival of the human race quest.

Remembering we all are pieces of the puzzle, which needs to be placed in its place to complete the plan in each ones quest.

The law of life, do we really think about what is required of us or are we moving along doing our own thing? But what is our thing? Many say I've learn from others who I believed to know the best way for me, while others say I am feeling my way through this life, and those who permit others to direct them in wrong decision making that messed things up badly for them and still others without a clue of what they are doing.

Because of the different opinions, in how one should live their lives, the law of life will force one to learn by experiences, if one refuses or unwilling to learn the proper way or by any other way the law enforces what is required to achieve the purpose goal.

There is something valuable, and that "time," we live for tomorrow by focusing on yesterday. So many people spend half of their time living in past pains or the moment in things that gives momentary pleasant. And the time keep going and going until there is no time left, to complete ones purpose and true destiny.

There are those who spend their time worrying about what could have been, if they had done this or the other. Time is being wasted on non-important things, one is not able to go back undo or to do things that was required for yesterday and do them today the time is lost, today it's time to do things required for today, what is done is done.

We are constantly faced with decision-making there are so much to think about in this quest, it's no wonder that many people is on the broader of insanity.

We can only say to our Source "Teach us to number our days with wisdom and focus our minds to apply that wisdom."

One of the most important things is to decide what you really want for yourself in time permitted. Time spend is the sure test of anything, whatever one's desire to achieve there must be time spend to prefect the worthy outcome. One cannot hurry and get anything of quality, it's the same with your life, one must be determines to accomplish whatever one desire for one's life that is constructive and positive for ones development.

The secret of time well spend is measures in ones successes in how well one succeed in the greatest responsibility entrusted to each of us that's the enfoldment of one's consciousness.

We have a responsibility to ourselves to unfold to the highs level possible, we are to utilize all the functional fabrications in the universe given us. The purpose of our lives is to develop and grow not only in the natural things for ones survival, this goes without saying, the greatest potential is for mankind to unfold ones spiritual, and mental bodies

Beyond what has been in the past through centuries of mistakes and pain.

Let each of us become all that one was intended to be and capable of being.

It seems difficult for some to be willing to step to the plate to act in the things that's good for them, only in the time of adversity is, one willing to act, why this?

There is power in learning and using your time wisely with confidence the end results will be worthy of all the efforts placed in it to achieve one's success in life.

The most valuable thing one has is ones faith in their Creator (God), who is giving it all.

After saying all this, we must understand, even in walking our own individual path to greatness each of us are on different level of growth, but all reach the same destination in their individual time of requirement. All must surrender to the up's and down's on their individual path of life to receive the goal of cultivation of our spiritual urgency.

When thoughts arise in many minds about the ones who are simply immoral and wicked in their activities, there is no spiritual urgency shown? Those individuals, are concentrated in activities of restlessness in the mind tries to find some try of peace from their action when there is none, and being lead by profound emptiness and as a result of their activities has cause suffering in self and to others as-well. These persons might frame themselves as doing what's right for them, but do they know what's right?

Why are we not the same; because of the hindrances and the unwholesome thoughts acted on. When people harbor harmful mental factors, they are on the lower-levels of development an pollute garment which needs to be wash a dirty cloth pick-up all the waste others have disregarded We all still recognize what we think and act on, but one must be mindful of our activities because of the results they will bring. As consciousness reveals the content of our thoughts that emerges of our energy with the guarantee of results to the situation or activity we can cause chaos in life, which is a form of evil. We attack and accept evil just as we attack good and harmony.

The precipitation, one can play with words to no end, but in reality we must remember there is a beginning and an end, meant a start and a completion to any plan.

Thoughts are seeds, feeling are incinerator which bring into manifest form into creation.

The constitution of the entire electronic force in the universe forms the body of God and is intelligent life. Thoughts and feeling are the building blocks of forms.

In order to create anything one must use their constructive faculty which is one's mind (conscious or unconscious), the feeling every thought form, known or unknown is being entertained within ones consciousness as one knows whatever thought and feeling are it will manifest in physical form by way of the laws of the universe in action, this why one must entertain harmonious and good thoughts.

Do you know that the mental patterns are energized by one's own emotional (feeling)? No thought is ever becomes a thing until it's coupled with the substance of feelings. This is why I inaccurate people to be mindful of their thoughts and feeling. A thought can only materially if the feeling are enforced behind the thought, now if one speak something negative and neutralize the thought before feeling come in to play that moment to its canceled the thought form and one is free, because it was not coupled with feeling. The universal law of asking forgiveness and the creative forces of thought has cleared it.

If mankind is to grow or evolve beyond the present state of their mind-set, one must work the requirement not just talk but action to achieve the knowledge about life understand the truth about oneself first. It can be difficult for many to change because many do not want change, so it's questionable how long it will take for those individuals.

No method of imperfection or its activities will change ones condition without the positive changes in one's mind-set for good activity and only one retrain one's own-inner thought patterns, and ones inner-conscious will be purity.

This physical world we see with our natural eyes is only appearances and everything in manifestation of the senses is but the externalized consciousness. One must go beyond the natural eyes to see the reality of things. By changing ones consciousness one will see the reality of life.

We live in a world of unlimited possibility of good things, knowing in reality all thing are good in there beginning. Somewhere along the way change took place that was not interred. It's time to touch and taste the imaging of our true beautify and let all out picture the fold of our true reality of being which is our god-person show it real face.

RIDDING THE SHAME

What and how humankind builds a world of shame? Was it, or Are we, pre-existed to be used as powerless-monkeys marching to the tone of the undeveloped individuals in morality and goodness? Are we beings with no individuality willing to follow every wish of groups who has no vision, those do not think before they act, or are we blindly obeying the powerful voices that rings out over the hills and valleys of life by various environmental modification of ideas occurring by observation or can we trace the chain back to the lack of intelligence, others words, and views of the human nature, as opposed to a Spiritual and Divine mind idea?

But at the same time many of us feel that life is worthy of our respect.

Are we listening to our inner-self or are we going with the flow led by others influences? Are we a people under the influence of Anesthesia, unable to feel, what is real, letting others block our mind transmission to the pain centers of reality of what is occurring in mankind development for good or minds that has been blocked and open to shameful activity which we see as shame?

What is mankind reality, can we examine the overall patterns as it begin to take shape within its confine process, step towards a unification of knowledge in matter or are we functioning under the influence of materialistic and barbarian ideas?

Are we intelligent human beings with cultural refinement or are we feeling useless and mindless creatures not understanding the need for knowledge of what is required for the purity and perfectness ones nature to act in one's life?

Countless years have come and gone as we see the slow progress in humankind evolvement of the real things in life. We know the Creative (Source) is still creating avenues for our growth and escape, divine love is continually working in our behalf.

We humans are like organisms that have been developed from two types of the lower forms that use only the barbarian and materialistic, which brings the ravages people in slow accumulation of small changes in evolution; perhaps if they would open-up to the light of truth it will bring one into the place of being in control of one's own destiny by stop listening to the lower influences of the surrounding social environment, just maybe change will occur.

Now on the other hand those who decided to be of the higher type developed the ability to survive as well as being the fittest, because they use the tools of the Divine Mind which it intelligence to reach the unknown of one's own destiny.

A few of us have learned the need to evolve to a Higher Consciousness, knowing it's the only way to Universal-Consciousness. By seeking this consciousness we recognize the important of life and use our time wisely putting aside all hatred and there causes, knowing Love is the key that will open all doors in life.

I guess you are wondering, what are the benefits in Universal-Consciousness; well for one thing everything below the Source of consciousness leaves space for mistakes which sets one back in their evolvement and slow their progress. Now those ones with the connection to the true Source Consciousness are working toward their ascension with the idea of not returning by reaching level 4 or 5 in the form of knowledge of the relative life on earth.

We who are on the ladder moving upward of life are becoming divine in nature.

The purpose for mankind is to share in the common goal of welfare of the world's inhabitants, in helping all by moving forward and upward in unison with the same mind for the whole of humanity to evolve. We are being given a chance to become one consciousness of good, above all being, self-conscious, knowing we are responsible for all affects others acknowledgement of one's moral responsibilities.

Because of one's intimate relations at times in situations it may become disturbing, but you're performances for good will reach out and influence others. And the quality of life becomes better and suitable for all.

Let's speak about the deeper truths of humankind, is most of mankind still thinking along the immature level about the mysteries of life and their purpose. Most people in their adult stage of life are so focus on survival and getting ahead in the world of materialism that their eyes are on only the superficial results in life.

To accomplish and recognize one's own individual self in fining the real meaning of life and further your journey toward ones superior level of thinking, one must put away the childish thinking.

One must acknowledge the Divine or Spiritual cord which emanates from the Source of creation of the three aspects in humans to the making a trinity within each of us, with the ability to interpenetrate the mysteries of our very existence.

There is much knowledge locked within the mental brain a force-field, which is trying to come forth if people would concentrated and study to permit the manifestation of that knowledge to come to its full potential. Each individual have control of their own responsibility to activate and simulate one's own awareness and to awaken one's mind to the levels of existing outside of one's own self the brain is only a tool.

One can only describe a small idea, of what makes a human being, we can depict that we are more than what we see with the naked eye with many of mankind it's much more than one beholds in the physical form. Human are like a tree standing in the light of the sun reaching for the blesses of the sun, mankind with its branches of different consciousness, attune to ones immortality through the waking conscious mind, the subconscious mind and ones super conscious mind, and as these branches join putting the aspects of mankind together with ones soul, personality and ones divinity it comes together.

When you can face the thoughts of being greater than just the body, than one's life become significant and worthy of the idea of everlasting and endless sweetness and serenity in all things.

A concentrated activity for the betterment of all of mankind and the creatures as well will bring the steps of progress toward humanity unification and one realizes no man is isolated from another. By concentrating ones efforts toward a unify people it increases and refines one receptivity to universal peace between all people.

Those who attain their minds to discover their actual oneness with humanity becomes self-realize and will permeate ever resistance which surround them and eliminate its operation.

If you believe in fate, then believe this; humankind will change for the better we may receive a little punishment for all the mistakes along the way. But humanity will survive and will be able to enjoy ones lives to the fully, when we turn from being self-destructive.

I would like to note here some important points the new views about life are nothing like the previous ones. Humankind views in the past are more of depend and self-control in the general stand-point, the people understood the need for assistants from others and now days everyone or all-most all people like to think they are doing their own thing, and many are morally out of control.

Another thing few people have respect for others desires, as long as it do not inter fear with them, understand what I am about to say, I myself do not have a personal opinion about how people live their lives, or and who they live with it is not my place to past-judgment on anyone. Each individual has the freedom of choice of whatever decisions they make for themselves, and what's fashionable to ones consciousness in everything. All activity is a repeat activity of the past, this is why society is not moving forward fast enough, it doesn't matter what the activity has been, it's still being repeated there is no change.

There is something I read in the papers about some Doctors, nurses and some pharmacist are refusing medical assist to certain people. One article incident when a lady requested an artificial insemination was denied because she was homosexual, the reason the clinic staff refuse they said, because of their own personal belief or religious they refuse their services to the lady. Question, what do the views of the staff have any concern in the desires of the young lady?

Are we the judgers, do we have the right to choice for others? Do not forget a person have the right to choice for their selves, we cannot choice for another person. Whatever the patient request, should not affect the staff, the Doctors and staff should feel impersonal to the request, as I said, no one has the right to interfere. If the staff is unwilling to service patients with ideas differ from their own then the staff should get jobs where other people will not have an effect on their views. If the staff members who refuse to act on the desires of the patients, a change, another line of work is in order. A Second incident where a young lady was raped on a date, turned away by a pharmacist in a drugstore, when she tried to get the morning-after pill.

Think about this would you be willing to have a child by someone who raped you, and knowing you would be looking in the face of a child representing that person? It is the policy for the pharmacist to make policy for the drugstore or is the owner in agreement with the pharmacist, the store is a public service and cannot discriminate there are laws to govern people in businesses who discriminate.

Third by no way less traumatic then the other two incidents, this young lady also had an incident with a pharmacist he wrongly assumed she was planning an abortion because she had a prescription for a drug that can be used for abortions. Her doctor found that the fetus she carried had no heart- beat or pulse, well it was dead she already had undergone a procedure by her doctor to remove it, but to complete the process she needed the drug, as she waited in the store she heard the pharmacist say, "I will not participate in an abortion, and I refuse." After setting there already heart full with grief for her lost, the pharmacist added to her grief. Ignorance binds one secure with an unwitting force, and can only be recognize by similarity.

There are those who will be argumentative to the statements, it maybe a disturbing subject for many, understand issues and challenges are not always black and white there are some shades of gray.

Everyone has a sense of life it's an integral part of one's make-up, although usually exist in ones subconscious. A person's sense of life largely determines upon ones major activity. The average person falls into one of two opposite categories, the objective rationalist or the mystical irrational.

The rationalist is conscious of what is real determine not to be concern with only ones self-interest, although they have depict as benevolent, and individualistic in a sense of life that characterized knowledge is the highest value one can achieve.

Sometimes there are certain individuals unwilling to accept they have no power to affect the outcome of others decisions. We as individual must remember each of us is an individual to one's self, and to take command of others mind and body is unacceptable. Appearances can be deciding as one shows itself to the outer world.

We find many things, which we felt to be basic realities of nature are just social fictions arising from common accepted or traditional ways of thinking about ones world.

The opposite's pole, one of being irrationality because one to view others as a ball to be push around and that you have the power to influence their lives, the difficulty comes in when you cannot accept that people are not puppets. The irrational person become preoccupied with their views, deeper troubles arise when one refuse to accept the fact that others people think differently by being one who is unreasonable and unwise confuses oneself and our fundamental relationship to the world around us causing fiction.

Most people are one of the two selfish or selfless; people subconsciously hopefully hold some thoughts of self-love, although we see outwardly only expresses of various selfless views deemed by virtuous tradition, political, theologians and social environment. It may seem that I am promoting selfishness, but think about, if one disregard oneself what type of life will you have or how can one be worthy of others caring for them? By being selfish in a constructive way all benefits, but if one gives all one has to others and lift with nothing, they both are losing.

One has to reject the destructive way of selfishness, and identify the honest view of selfishness, it can be steps toward self happiness and personal prosperity, by giving some of what you have but not all, now both are half way to your goals, not saying one should not give to the poor and others in need, but to know where to draw the line, all is being said, not to jump in the boat of poverty with them. Selflessness is what most people think is a noble thing, or is it really?

Impression, see it working to destroy ones state of mind, it makes one to sacrifice. As it been said to take from Peter being oneself to pay Paul being another which is the responsibility of Paul who may have created or produced the situation in the first place and others should not be put in that position to be selfless, it primarily wrong, which has been placed on mankind that says, "God likes a cheerful giver," how can you be cheerful by taking a loss?

Do you think God want you in poverty because you did not use common sense?

There are all sort of causes need attention, but you cannot support all causes it will bring an undo sacrifice, when we make mistakes in judgment it can be hard to recover. That why we must think before acting it means you do care about self. It a place to keep burdens off one's self. Want you to think about how people use different concerns to extract your valuables in the name of needs. The nations use selfless sacrifice of body and spirit for fighting wars, and man's love of nature and the need for survival in the form of fighting inflation, etc., the states use fighting poverty, fighting drugs, and maybe pollution, and religious groups, say they are fighting for all sort of noble causes, many are doing so with an air of self-righteousness.

Back to the young ladies, who needed assistance but was turn down by medical staff and pharmacists without a clue of the lady situations and reasons why, but made decisions in regard to their care using their so call religious views as the reason for their decisions.

The lack of understanding about any issue is a crime toward any individual.

There are those who make a career from other people willingness to be selfless individuals who are sacrificing for traditions, the results sacrifice of one's growth and happiness because of not rejecting those of false intent.

Humankind nature is to evolve and learn survival skills, to see the world around us that is within it. Mankind has the ability to think and reason choosing to integrate those concepts, which represents the condition. The logical integration of concepts is called reasoning; man's reasoning ability is his survival.

When mankind undermines ones reasoning ability it becomes inactive.

Integration of one's conscious mind will reduce one's efficacy, well -being, self-worth and happiness, all of which results in poor quality of life.

Reasoning is that part of man's nature which gives one elevation to ones values

Yet acting on fully integrated honesty, not reasoning itself is the basic moral act. Reasoning can be beneficial or destructive, if you want to say, moral or immoral whatever the conscious mind entertains. If for any reason one entertains thoughts of dishonestly in using one's reasoning ability it become harmful and immoral. So you see there are two sides to reasoning.

Back to the young ladies, the people who denied them the use of medical assistance using their personal views as their reason for not serving the ladies, no one has the right to control another life, the knowledge of free will or choice of the individual, is out the window, it only shows ignorance in use of their power to control others situation.

Many religious groups discovered ages ago how to route their power of guilt onto innocent people with values, but the people, they blindly follow their religious leader.

The church have become increasingly preoccupied with building large organizations with the need for material and noticeably.

Augustine started the promotion of guilt through his books, laying the foundation for great oppressions. He converted to Christianity in 383 A.D the major book by him, the "City of God," speculated how babies mighty are born from women unconquered by lust and sex. Disregard for the women and the respect for the creativeness of life. Augustine became a master achiever and gain respect of the Christian movement of that era, creating problems where none existed. Augustine destroyed values rather than create them, but the people still accepted him.

By 585 A.D. the Catholics argued that women did not have moral souls and debated if women were even human beings. Women became pieces of disposable property. By 904 the clergy and pope turned to prostitutes and neurotic sex, practicing incest and was lecher with children, can you see the sins against God and mankind did not come from outside the church but within the heart of what is regarded as God's house.

Believe it or not its history of the church, the information can be found if one wants to know the truth; I did research for information on the statements I make.

The Catholic clergy sanctioned different immoral acts, like prostitution for their purpose, and put their values in the closet when it benefit them whine along without values in acts of even forced rape or sadistic sex, they regarded the act as not a serious offense, all the real penalties were placed on the women. Women were considered as property of the men, and the church sanctioned wife beating, men were only fined by the church for killing women; there were no laws to protect the women from the men. You would think since no law in the land worked for the women, that the church would be different by being the so -call house of God?

Even this day and time we have problem in the protection of women, remember the things sanctioned by the church and the root of that thought is still in many today.

Now do you see the need of ridding mankind of its shame and this is a shame?

Not until the 1500 A.D. did a small change took place by some of the noblemen with the trend toward good and beauty in women. But the pope attacked the ideas by setting up a new breed of malefactors; two theologians enforced the activity, by Jacob Springer and Henry Kramer acting as inquisitors. Springer and Kramer wrote a widely influential book dealing with the evil of women and witchcraft, which lead to burned to death tens of thousands of innocent women.

Why hang on every word that comes from the church views, think for yourself, if you do not believe what I have written research the information for yourself. I want you to question, what I've said and think about who wrote the laws that you live by. You have a mind use it for your clarity. "Please research what I found in my research."

Enough of the church for now read more in my next book on the subject of relationships between men and women, back to the main subject.

Question: Are we humans so blind to the true needs of our fellowmen and other forms of life that we degrade Life itself? Has the flow of life Energy stop reaching the minds of mankind to maintain the purpose?

All human doubts and fears of a new age of recovery are just words if people do not act on change in their own lives first, tremendous things can be done, if you make sincere effort to change and maintain that change with peace and harmony in one's own consciousness. Using that saying, "there is only God in action in my mind and body."

The habit of humans is they look for imperfection, having doubts about life, using the words, "I can't, or she or he can't" and so on, each time you dwell on the thought of an unproductive thought you create and give power to that thought.

Now let me suggest that you acknowledge at that time or moment its power, but from the moment on it has no power, this is a way, and you can set into motion for your freedom, protection and to receive the blessing in the renewing of your mind and consciousness.

Continuing now to float, the rocks gently, drifting deeper and deeper until your mind approaches the truth about humankind, his past and present conditions which in time will destroy us if we do not change for the better. For a while you may surround yourself with thoughts of harmony and peace, but will you continue to demonstrate what you now feel?

As you learn to use your mind more effectively, you will become able to manifest the qualities of that harmony and peace towards every living thing. You will feel yourself that part which is body charging you with pleasure giving rise to a good deal of happiness, so that you do want to experience it and feel, its strength, it weaknesses, and be willing to submit to the charge to change.

We are extensions of the Godhead who incarnates onto the earth plane with the make-up of soul, personality, mind, emotions and a physical body. With the purpose to evolve and do battle between ones higher self and lower self or you can say ones ego self and divine self.

To achieve the highest stage in life, which brings the divine self in place of total control, one must achieve the constructive attributes aspects.

One must awake to the power of purpose and will, with the willingness to organize one's life in a concrete science of knowledge and order with devotion to what is important in life.

The only different between the higher and lower sides of an individual is ones awareness of the need for improvement of their lower self to reach their true existence in order to get the best results of one's choices.

By attaining this realization and going on living as one desires knowing one is free to do just exactly as one likes, being aware of the false freedom of doing as one like, knowing the result may not be in ones best interest. The best way to attain this realization is to let one self free to remember ones ignorance's and foolishness of the past and try to make your self God like by simply becoming a perfectionists.

Yes, I say be a perfectionist, that my opinion I believe it's the way to get the best result, but in reality its all-inclusive, it does not depend on thinking any special kinds of thoughts or having a particular feeling ever in the background of one very soul. One is free to think of anything and nothing at all.

We are free to feel both compassion and anger whatever the experience one knows that whatever the direction one chooses it's still in harmony with the one that includes all directions and all opposites.

Sometimes it's hard to face reality, but it's true that all is God's directed in life and some kind of rapport with the spiritual in a sense, causing all ways to be included in God. As we begin to understand we wake up to ones freedom to be alive, right or wrong ones activities whatever they maybe are by God's permission, so it's God's directing all directions and all opposites as well.

But it's up to us to decide which direction this freedom given by God's power is to be channeled. Basically we have the power to process and direct by the Divine Source

(God's) power, to develop toward higher levels of perfection in mind or step down to because a spiritual separation from God's divinity and one's own divine self.

The idea of any kind of separation from the influence of the Godly spiritual directing power would be a terrible blow for me as an individual, being that God's Power of Love is our safety net.

Knowing the spiritual guide will carefully observe our every activity; it would be a very serious undertaking to approach any situation without asking for guidance of the Divine Presence to show the way for our success.

It's a comfortable security in knowing each moment and experience an image wills describes meaning and has greatest effectiveness inducing as an altered state of consciousness for good.

You find yourself going deeper developing the capacity to experience riches you have never dreamed of the subjective realities will stimulate your imagination by the eliciting of vivid images evocative of the creative process of your mind. Going deeper and deeper into your divine self, one can reach the most profound and expanded awareness achievable to receive the comprehensible meaning permitted of God's intentions.

It's when one receives their first real insight, knowing what a person must do must come from ourselves to become that God-Person which is the final evolution.

Let's look back from where we came from, until the first millennium B.C. mankind along with all other primates functioned by mimicked or learned reactions. Because of mankind larger brain, mankind brain was complex this gave them an edge over the other primates; humankind learned guilty and developed a coherent language as a form of communication. As humankind begins to communicate with each other and societies were developed.

The fundamental need of the human recall supposes everything in us that is transfused by our knowledge belongs to the past.

TRADITIONAL SACRIFICES

Many who have known deep within that it's time for change and we must let the enfoldment of love take place in society now. Everything possible of the old ways has been done and we still are creating wars and chaos, all of this activity is still hardening people hearts and minds.

No outside forces are the blame, no evil, no angels, no extraterrestrials etc., humanity is the blame, and these who activities are evil are the blame for the chaos and wars they create by their power to create.

People are not willing to sacrifice the old ways of thinking and reach for new ways for their betterment. Understand at this point in our history a change is a must in order. Millions of years have come and gone and we still are holding on to old views that do not work in our best interest in the times, do you believe there come a time where there will be no more time?

Many years there has been substantial misunderstanding concerning the good and bad nature of people, out of ignorance people were doing things and that seem right to them, and no one question them on the situation and others followed their led.

To emphasize, being ignorance of a thing does not make you exempt from the penalties you will be responsible to pay. All journeys in life we are responsible of our own journey, and what we decide determines if it goes upward or downward in our contemplation from moment to moment. It simply is not acceptable for one being ignorant of a situation in regard to one's own life; I am not talking about the ones who are mentally challenged.

Its human nature to want to know why and how of what brings things and conditions into existence? Yes, we learn through our senses and the unfolding of mind, which bring forth ideas into the field of consciousness to act on, although this is a wonderful thing, but how many permit others or to think on a given thing without the opinion of someone else?

For the sake of argument, knowing we learn though our intelligences by the connection with nature and associative persons who are creative in whatever their minds are focus on and also the creatures by intentionally or unintentionally connect. It is only by one's mind we accept what is being given.

We as humans may not know the different between many things in this world we live in, but we try to know as much as possible in the shortest time, this can be a plus. Although what we precept as truth may not be true, but we try to get the truth from all contacts in life and this can be a blessing or can cause problems.

The highest steps that mankind has made is when after many millions of years was the dawning the unfolding of their mental faculties. Many have advanced to the level of consciousness of the "oneness of all", knowing there is only one reality that Life of all is "One".

First in perception the "One," it's Love, brings one's ability mentally to determine what sensations will rule at each moment in one's life, will it be ones emotions rule of anger, hate, love, ambition, or jealousy etc., the very fact that we have come to the place that we can examine and consider what we are doing is right or wrong, we have come to the place of accountability for all our actions.

The average person recognizes their strong and weak points in their character, and they know on the average what is right and wrong in the eyes of society.

One has a mental picture of what is required of them, but instruct of cultivating proper character, one overlook the possibilities and practice the old way of thinking.

The majority of the views of the old way are blinding the people and some of the new ways are no better, so what are we to do, ask for divine direction in all our activities from the life giver (god).

Let look at the different concept about simply ones eyesight, we perceive the enjoyment of what our eyes can see, although it's been said that the eyes are limited and only shows impresses of colors and objects of matter. However if one uses ultraviolet lighting certain minerals beyond the nude eye will show amazing things.

For instances rocks show luminescent colors and when the light is removed it returns to its original coloration, the same is if one place a rock under a microscope and magnified the rocks image it will reveal all that is limited to the nude eye. The nude eye only registers degrees of the creative vibrations of all things seen in creation.

The abstract expressionists artist characterize emancipation from brush sticks freely developing shapes and designs representing a physical object or concept, in many colors as it cultivates one's own creative nature through, as different form its normal awareness. And as we observances the pictures we develop our own opinions and meaning to what is being precedence in the work of art, for all people have different views. The final impressions are individually decides. Remember, all of us view according to our different mentalist and moods.

The sciences have taught us a great deal about the intricate mechanisms of our physical universe that we are to appreciate those underlying powers.

So without ones sight one cannot know the differences in colors or the light of day from the darkness of night. So in trying to customary habits of the old ways in putting on ones coat left arm first, and then right arm, it boils down to what one is taught in their impressionable years and ones mental development over the years

Many have become mere slave to customs, creep and sects. The wise person sets oneself apart from the ignorance's of others. If one let the soul unfold and ones spirit will gradually manifest itself in consciousness beyond the old traditional views and there will be less of one's true-self is sacrificed.

Let's move to another condition many overlook, for years people talk of ignorant savages ones who believe in many gods and bloody sacrifice of their fellow humans to a god of some kind. But in realty there are people in this day and age doing the same to a materiality god, by waging war to gain their material wealth from others.

Many are unconscious of their underlining belief in those same gods although somewhat differently. Think of the ones who seek power and control others land, wealth, and bodies. That has been a tradition for many nations and empires. They will clothe these gods with human attributes in unproductive fashion and in a sense.

They tell themselves and you they are justified in their actions. Some have courage to ask God for assistance in these try of acts. The bottom line ignorant and foolishness, is not overlooked, really hoping God will overlook it by saying it's a "holy war," all of which to clear their conscious for the injustice toward their fellowman, wanting to believe it's okay to kill and by asking God using the deities to enforce their views and wants on others, with the thought one is exempt from the law of cause and effect, not so no one is exempt from the laws of the universe.

What makes it so unbelievable some really believe it themselves that there is holy wars among people, think about it are you holy have you unfolded to the place your world is full of love and harmony and if so you would not want to war with others.

It's been a tradition down through time for people believe that people are your friends or your enemies.

Let's change the subject a little, some people imagine that God is the one who divides people into different groups, it's not God it's because of the particular conceptions of people, how they want to worship also some imagine they are the chosen ones or special favorite ones of God. In being those favorite of god feel they can wage wars with others unflavored ones without reaping what one sowed.

Back to the main subject, all people have the same make-up in general with the ability to change at will and only the true Source remains the same in showing Love to all creation.

If you really look at it, there is no large "I" and little "You" it just you and I, we all came from the main Source. We are all a part of the plan of life and we all are working our part in that plan individually, for the benefit of life, but as one.

We need to stop thinking if we do battle with others and use the deity as a tool to deceit they will triumph and overcome their enemies, and with thoughts of being right to justified their actions even to the place of killing women and children, using the name "Holy War," understand there is nothing holy about war. Many believe God delight in human blood flooding the land, not so.

The ignorance of traditions can restrain a nation and its people from making progress. All nations have some savageness in them you do not need to become a part of others views and desires, only try to unfold yourself and be the best that you can be.

It's a new age now, and it's time to remove the old traditional habits which cause destruction of life.

The human race needs to raise to the highest and greatest in all its concepts of life, in general terms build on new and better concepts of life.

Let's go back a little in history in battling with ones enemies, in history all nations have acted in battle of some kind and they all believed they were right in their activity, but is it right to take life from another? You are not the giver of life then you should not be the taker.

The feeling of being alive is just as strong in the next person as it is in you. When doing battle the emotion is high and others are pushing you to move forward in the action. The purpose of such activity is to show your willingness to destroy another for a cause that only satisfies the ones who believe in that cause, whether it's right or wrong.

When an individual who has killed another human being has accepted his new status as a person that assisted in destruction of another person opportunity to move to the next level of evolvement in that body and the person must come back and do it all over again.

The purpose of all of us is to assist in getting rid of the intense desires of destruction in other words to aid and be a reminder of the importance in seeking higher qualities of one's life. We would ask you to remember the body is a mirror of one's own reality.

Normally a person reach a higher level of consciousness of how life could be, as one comes in contact with their true self and through arranging the patterns of their existence by learning the purpose and completing the lessons in this life. At that point it will be clear of what desire that bound them to the battle mentality.

Where there are thoughts of rebellion of new ideas and a new way of living judgmental views of the new verse tradition that only slows ones progress.

Many wish others to stay in the traditional confinement, suggesting the new ideas are not for them and the mission is complete, which caused many to be driven into a state of mental apathy and non-productive nests.

One must avoid the pitfalls, do not allow yourself to fail yourself, wrong instruction supports failure. But take the steps leading up to the realization of one's true self, and remember you are an individual with a mind that expands the self, if you let it.

The highest step outside that of one's oneness with all life is the reality of the "I" and we as individuals have the gift of choice. The greatness of each individual is to unfolding into consciousness, seeing the vision of a peaceful people in their own personal expression through their words and activities.

The greatest price a person pay is when they follow others path and not their own.

To advance one's own soul is to separate and identify the real part of oneself from the group, the collective thought pattern which fails.

How can this be expressed in words, for it's hard to fit ones concept; let's say it like this; "realizing the self as we know all of the visible world is found in the one life, one force, one substance, one existence, one reality, and we are all one, experiencing a different form of expression of that One.

Even though we are one in individuality we gain character from our surroundings, still we must fulfill our own individual destiny, to unfold to the higher levels of evolvement. The Source of power to give knowledge will guide and direct us and it will ensure that the truth of what must be known will reach each one of us to reveal our true self and purpose.

Traditions are engraved in every cultural activity and seem to be right because that is what one learns. If you look like an animal and act like one then you must be one. One doesn't have the insight into the present or the past to shape the right method to live by because there is no variety to choose from.

We eat, drink, and sleep and purchase whatever we desire and most of all we educate ourselves to be able to do at will; the beauty of it is we do much of what we desire. All of which comes from the influence of one's culture background one lives.

Today, as a result of the inter action of different cultures an increasing of awareness of the importance of change for the better for one's life is in play. One may be confuse between the old way and the stimulation of certain new ideas. By exercising ones choose as an individual one improves.

The ultimate goal is to stimulate the mind that brings your own mind the two point, where you think for yourself and just maybe a change is in order for your life from the old ways of tradition. Let the higher forces of one's nature stimulate and educate so you can become one of the elite who are no longer enslaved by traditions that control the growth of a nation of people.

From today, all responsibilities of your future are in your own hands, traditional habits service no real purpose, if they are not good ones. Many are tied up and have trouble grasping the important of the process of freeing one's mind from the confusion of many in the past.

Many traditions build nothing they are maintained through habit, they are lifeless and stagnated. Looking back from an open mind point of view many are in their personal worlds, which are just like a factory habit working on an assembly-line doing the same thing each day in the same old way, no change day after day, no growth, no change, no progress and no real purpose of their own, just following along.

One must embrace change, and develop their own dreams, discover the ability to trap the real Sources to permit the overflowing enjoyment of self -empowerment.

Understand the powerful forces of knowledge of any given thing dictates ones patterns, the emotions, mental, physical and spiritual states, all the struggles while trying to satisfy ones craving, even in the form of dislike, hatred, resentment etc., are rewarded in the personal weaken of the individual.

On the other hand if one use the powerful forces in a positive fashion then one can suppress the unruly hungers and craving that blinds the insight to true freedom of ones being, which releases one from tradition.

CRIME OF SOCIETY

This may seem odd to many of what I am about to say; prior to mankind embryo stage there was a god embryo. Each human being first receive a part of this god's embryo, which gave humans the unlimited power to chose ones channel or parents to enter the earth plane for their learning and retrieve. Humankind originally was created to mirror the divine forces, being that god's embryo exists in everything in the universe, along with their biological factors we came into true manifested form.

As we live in the earth plane we unfold to express ones desires in these five senses and perhaps beyond our present five. Even though we are on the earth plane, we must still live on a higher evolved level to learn to live in full consciousness of both the physical and spiritual levels hoping not to be in the shadow of the mirror that reflect the dark side of one's nature. Although one receives energies, which flow through our planetary atmosphere, we also receive it from the small's blade of grass and power from the ethers that surround us. And transmit them into the physical form and one's personal atmosphere with their influences.

When one permits the dark shadow side to seize control the patterns of one's desires, that energy becomes the individual controlling consciousness, end turns become overshadows ones fallacious given a non-constructive results of energy one creates for oneself, and others by being power sets.

One can achieve and unfold the powers of the unseen potion of the universe that surrounds us and have use of these powers for constructive or destructive purposes. Understand this power is a free gift from ones

Creator, the power of chose or free will makes one responsible for all their own activities. Knowing the real purpose of free-will was to enable humankind to become as god's, by seeking ones spiritual perfection.

We all have chooses in life, our own lives, no one can blame anyone else for chooses that we make ourselves. In any undertaking after the age of understanding of right and wrong we as individuals are responsible for our own actions whether accomplishments or defeat, to our true purpose.

There maybe some controversy in what I am about to say, but it will not alter the truth in any way. Everyone has free will in all areas of life because in that free-will came an openness to use that force in whatever way possible, given it command to choose whether they shall serve the upward or the downward path for their lives. Believe it or not no one can make the chose for other persons in reality they must choose their own path.

For those who choose the upward path to divine enlightenment to god have the clarity and sincerity of mind to reach the relative perfection required of the Creator in doing so they know they can call for assist of the higher powers in every manner that is permissible.

The ones who sincerely seek the upward path know if they call on the laws which governs the universe and ask for the law of forgiveness each and every day not forgetting to give thanks and praise for having come to the reality and conscious understanding of the God power that works within them, also in knowing the creative powers in life are continuously flows ceaselessly on through one's life.

On the other hand when a person chose the downward path as one entertain discordant in one thoughts and actions the law of attraction occurs. Ones mainstream of life patterns develop and continue to build in the non-constructive activities and those who do harmfulness to others and most of all to one's own soul evolvement.

Many are moving downward only to fine the need to move upward in order to save ones own soul from destruction, there is a measure of time for each of us to come to the highest point of creation, that being where we started in the prefect place of God's grace and love. Many think they are okay.

Not so dear ones, when those who are not showing improvement or willing nests to unfold on the upward path there will be a time required and if one has not moved upward or forward in the light of God their time will cease and they will cease to be, no eternal life or immortality for them.

In reality when a person is on the downward path it becomes a crime towards the individual very soul evolvement and the punishment or penalty is to cease from beings permitted to evolve, as if you never existed.

In the mean time while the individual thinks life is a game or they think there is time the time is running out. Going downward one will continue until one arrive to find all the non-productive activities have structured their outer consciousness and the only thing for them is to simply ingrate in the gratification of one's physical appetites and pleasures sensation created by the lower consciousness of what we call animal form of a human being, but in reality I do not like using animal as an example for low-mindedness in people because some animals are highly evolved.

In using their free will in the law of expression, even if they have the right, but what if it affects others, what of the rights of others, now what?

Then it becomes a problem, which develops into a crime and punishment is required The power of knowledge of oneself with the ability to chose one of the two opposites, is would be more ideal for one to chose the upward Good qualities instead of later trying to reverse the undertaking one have placed on oneself.

It been said, that to learn by experience is the best teacher and self-knowledge or to be conscious of one's self-experiences are the reasons one must go though the experiences and learn from them.

My view, one need not experience all things in order to learn, there are many experiences others persons have is enough to learn by, just visual you know many experiences are not for everyone to experience and my own experiences have been enough for me to learn, knowledge shows direction.

An example; in my view, one's ability to learn from others experiences, if I see a person fall in a hole to their death, I do not need to jump in the hole to know I will also die. We can learn by seeing the man in the hole. We learn from others in every form of life, and develop character by the influences of others, whether good or bad.

The link between people even if they do as they choose, one cannot get away from some influences, they are always present, but it's a matter of what one allow into one's life that can choose the path they will follow.

Yes, many are weak non-productive in many areas but in the long run the individual must make decisions for themselves, when the time comes the earned right to choose freely for one's life. Ones most powerful tool is to control one's own situation by choice. As one step into the path of right or wrong he controls, which is focus on and by align with it, the choice will enter one's life to assist or destroy.

If dishonesty is focus eventually choices of destructive activities will lead to the criminal mind patterns and knowing the criminal minded person is guilty of the destroying of it own life first, and then the life and values of others.

Many people only see the criminals who are robbers of homes and banks, and the people on the streets and or the killers of the bodies and mind.

The undercover criminals are those who are masters of deception that undermine individuals and even themselves.

There are many crimes against humanity, not all are from one on one situation.

There are crimes against oneself, if one stand unyielding to what is wrong for them with a firm determination to use substances that is known to kill, and they use it anyway with knowledge, what can I say? "That is self."

One must not yield to or embrace the limitations of short moments of false pleasures that only give confidence during the arising enjoyment, afterward the return of conditions and or the state of depression to dictate ones weakness outwardly being fully conscious that it is acting as the substance dictates, and accomplishing its goal to seize the individual very forward desire, you become, a victim of your own making and that is a crime.

The power is within you, take a single moment, listen and try to feel the truth within yourself, once you feel your life stream as boundless the power will come for victory, although you have had great success and confidence in your day to day activities, but you have not gain momentum for the containment of the good things in life other then survival which is only the materials or matter of life.

We know there are many millions of people desire a good life, and desire wholeness, but where are the boundaries in activities. In nature we understand the path to wholeness embodies the impulse towards the spiritual quest, which brings strength and all types of fertility.

The only way to completeness is to receive the massages, which brings sacred gifts and signals warnings, with discriminative minds and with spiritual conscious to the insight and ones true enfoldment to the true reality of life.

The love which has been given to us humans from the Source of life separates us from disruption giving liberation to break free from constricting identification with only the material realty and to experience the real-world of the cosmic reality.

We humans must become warriors for what is right towards our fellow-humans and other living forms of this world. Initiating a partnership to open the gateway to inspires ones-self and others in the celebration of what real life is from our births and our deaths.

There is a sacred marriage other than the marriage between a man and women, this is symbolically in its form; one may have struggled to know ones path or purpose in life and the life one is living does not satisfies, and you feel frighten in need of comfort. We can look to the Source with a clear mind and willing heart, to be a dictator of ones wills understandings the need for balanced. It indicates a need to become aware of your inner-being, the divine part of you. The sacred marriage union is the upper and the lower become one in action, but the higher part being in control, there is only "One" the Soul has taken it rightful place with the Spiritual part uniting all of you.

And So It Is

The Criminal mind

The criminal minded are oppose to the purpose of life, not only human life, other, life forms as-well. They are the most ignorant of all of mankind, placing their effects to receive false prosperity and power through deceptive means, hoping this will make them happy, in what they perceptive happiness to be. Through whatever means or substances possible, enforcing their so-call power to convey directly or indirectly initiated force to support the draining of life's values and happiness from honest citizens and other life forms.

The quality of life one has in one's social surroundings and world environment causes one to fear the moment and the future, people who do crimes against humanity and or others forms of life are people who fear the reality of the relativity of not knowing what today or tomorrow going to bring in this lives. Fear of life's past experiences bring forward in ones mind the unstableness of ones life, knowing the chances for life to be a continuing of unsecured life experiences, they are fearful about life in their reality.

Anyone who desires more clarity to this information can research for one-self into the following statements to be true or false the proof is in ones search. In thinking about this just be open and receive the importance of what is given.

There are masters of deception and they work hard to undermine the people they target every day. These people are not your everyday contact in the general public but people that you may look up to as leaders of society. Think about the ones so-called intellectuals and spiritual, the government officials. Let me make it clear I am not saying all leaders are deceptive, but the scale is unbalance. We Know there are good speaker doesn't make it right, think about it, for whom? It's plane that the politicians-Presidents, Senators, Congressmen and other leaders in government and power to govern the people interest, many of the theologians- ministries, clergymen, priest, rabbi and other those who hold diplomats of official administer and the social intellectuals, are keeping some of the truth from those willing to accept what is others give them without question in order to keep peace and keep in line with their personal ambition.

First let's make it clear, I am not saying all individuals in these positions are criminal minded there are good and bad in all fields of work. This target is on those who knowingly use deception for their own personal gain. Ones, who do wrong to other people with no concerns directly or indirectly by their activities, which will affect others, then their selves,

Many may think the truth will work things out in time, but that's not true always, things can get worse. Decision-making is a large part of society problems people in the power-set can make wrong decision purposely. Those who make policies that affect millions of people, these persons who are running our government the so-call leadership. This country has been bankrupt for decades having no substance like Gold and Silver to back it, the only asset it has are the people and our labor, thought our taxes.

I have a question for you why are we required to record a birth or death?

Why do you think it's a must to have birth certificates and social serenity cared?

We are collateral on the interest on the loan to the World Banks.

The U.S. Treasury paid with more and more of their wealth of Gold so the structured inevitability soon transpired- the treasury of U.S. government was empty the deft was greater than ever in 1913 until 1933 U.S. paid interest with Gold and property this mean that the Crown laid claim to everything. In exchange for use notes belonging to bankers who created them out of nothing based on credit we are force to repay in substance our labor, property land productivity, Business, and resources in ever increasing amounts. Place research this information for yourself as I did

Back to the treasury, they issued the bond on our Birth certificates and bond was sold as securities exchange and brought by FRB, which then use it as collateral to issue for the Fed's as the depository trust corporation. By the way the Federal Reservoir is not government, it's a proprietor corporation.

We became the transmitting unity for the transmissions of human energy the US Government in order to provide necessary goods of its Citizens as payment for the debt (Bankruptcy). As, far as the commercial bond is concern is makes us all "Chattel" property and Slaves to the country bankruptcy. You think people would have change over the years but we have people doing the same things in this day and age covering up wrong, those who cover-up wrong decisions, which cause this country to be in Bankruptcy. And those government officials who make decisions to benefit large companies only to see dollar signs for their own individual benefit from these companies now and the future.

Understand, Sovereign American and the sole creation of these agencies was for the purpose of collecting the debt. The U.S. A. is a corporation owned by England-The Crown- the Vatican. The 14th Amendment to the Constitution of the U.S.A. was in order to enslave those who contract with the state thereby giving up their natural-born freedom in exchange for so-called benefits.

Check this out, the private meet of during the administration of Woodrow Wilson –President-1913-1921, making every American to register their biological property (that is ones family members), a system designed to keep track of the people, by their birth and their death. Think about it, how would the country be able to get the money to pay the debt?

First understand I am not talking about all government officials, only the ones that do business with shameful activities which deceive the people who placed them in their positions with lies saying they're for the people.

The Governing Houses Gangsters doesn't necessarily mean the president, but it could, some things about some of the former presidents that have been unveil which is unsuited for one in their position. Knowing those are those who are secure in misusing us in our growth toward the so-call American dream.

Many are going to continuously be enslaved in ignorance's in the so-call logic in opinions of others (social peers) or those being concern about popularity behind other opinions. In so doing they dishonor themselves and others. If you desire to know more on the subject please investigate all that has been said here. What I desire is for all to be informed, people's mind must be willing to open to the truth so one as an individual not be imprison by the defense mechanism of old control tradition.

Every benefit you believe you receive from the state whether U.S. or Canada is at a cost huger tan you could ever imagine unless you can keep it all separated.

One example is buying property there a tax-called a lawful tax and its legal, which release ones title to the government corporation and leaves you with only equitable title the right to use, not own, and for the use you pay a user tax, which is every tax, income, sales, property, etc. As opposed to lawful taxes excise and impost so that it doesn't appear that the government now own that you won't suspect it is placed in a name resembles your own that won't be suspected.

We look to the government officials as the ones who will protect the people of this country, not to use them for personal gain which cause pain and suffering for others. I will go into more detail later on in this chapter of the government house gangster.

First let us go back to another example; take the ones who developed the Constitution as it was originally intended by the ones who wrote it. Talk about division, the nation was divided in the beginning and it is still divided in part today. The people were separated into two groups of citizens.

First we must define the original Constitution of the two citizens. In 1787 the definition and intend of the Constitution was to describe a free born Citizen of the several states. The 14th Amendment added a second (2) distinct meaning to the phase. Now the phase "citizen of the United States has two separate and distinct meaning.

Let's really look at the meaning and intend of the ones who wrote the Constitution in 1787, understand their only concern was for free born so call "white" individuals in the several states. Now notice I said "free born," there were some white's enslaved in that day and time.

Let's examine the original intend it was for the free born whites "Citizens" notice in Article 1, Section 2, (capitalize of the "C") and numerous other section each time with capitalization, this referred to the sovereign political body of the state Citizens of the several states under Article IV. Understand there are different citizen in the Constitution. Although Congress utilized the same term with a small "c" to distinguish the federal citizen in the 14th Amendment, Congress and most of the judiciary have acknowledge the amendatory act cannot alter the original intent of the Constitution. *(1.) A free born white is a state Citizen in the several states, an individual whose inalienable rights are recognized, secured, and protested by the various states constitution against state actions and against federal intrusion by the Constitution for the United States of America of 1787. (2.) The 14th Amendment brought in the second class citizen, notice with a small "c" federal citizens, these are what is called juristic person, or a citizen of foreign or interstate, commerce, granted privileges that are almost equal to the white Citizen. These second- class citizens are subjects of Congress under their protection as a resident of a state, person enfranchised to the federal government (the incorporated United States defined in Article 1, section 8, Clause 17). Thus the federal citizen is a taxable entity such as any other corporation and subject to pay an excise tax for the privileges that has granted them.*

In researching information understand they all have a different language and specific meaning attached, like the "person" as defined in the so-call 14th Amendment. It does not mean or includes everyone, as you are lead to believe. There are several court cases that define who are that specific "person," and of those cases is Van Altenburg v. Brown, 43 cal 43. A statement, by, chief justice Taney in the case of Dared Scott v. Sanford, 19, 393, and 422 in the defining the term "person" the Judge stated persons, who are not recognized as Citizens. More information can be had in American and Ocean Ins. Co. v. Canter, 1 Pet. 511, which also distinguishes "person" and "Citizen".

These were the persons that were the object of the 14th Amendment, to give to this class of native born "persons" who "resident" in the union of the United States citizenship, and authority place other than the white race within the special category of "citizen of the United States."

To vanquish the statement in Dared Scott, supra, that only white people were citizens, and all other persons were only "residents" without citizenship of the States, Congress then passed the Civil Rights Act of 1866, 14 STAT.27. The act of Congress called the Civil Rights Act, 14 U.S. Stats. At Large, p. 27, which was the forerunner of the 14th Amendment, shows intend of Congress.

Now the term "United States," has three (3) different distinct, and separate jurisdictional meaning. You can fine the meanings in Hooves and Allison co. v. Evart, 324 U.S. 652. Each of these definitions has completely different jurisdictions and cannot be mixed. So if in doubt ask.

The Federal Constitution can only be applied and used against the federal government. The Bill of Rights (Articles in addition to the original First 7 Articles) was written strictly as a limitation on the federal government, to protect the Citizens of the several States from the federal government. The federal constitution does not apply to states actions against states citizens.

The 14th Amendment, since 1969 has allowed limited application of the federal constitution only to the extent that congress has seen fit to grant as a privilege to be applied against states governments for the specific protection of the 14th Amendment citizens of the United States.

By the federal government not being within the Common law Writ under Article 1, section 9, or the constitution for the U.S. of America (1787), which is available only to white common law states citizen: and under the writs statue, which is for all others, and congress has allowed only limited applications and which can be denied for any reason. There are two (2) writs of Habeas Corpus for the state of California: (1.) Under the Constitution Article 1, section 11, which is the white common law state Citizen; and (2.) In the Penal Code, Title 12 chapter 1 section 1473, which was enacted 23 years after the creation of the state of California in 1872.

This subject matter was given to inform you of how people can appear to be pursuing a valid approach to unify people but the truth is not there when one makes a division or different in citizens not understanding people are just people human being's it's not the coloration of one's skin or in ones language or original country from which one come that makes a different, but the mind-set and the character of the individual that makes the different.

Lets look at the different agencies that was developed to control the people in this country and some of the foreign countries, Breton Woods agreement 1944 to develop of the International Monetary fund and from there all the foreign agencies, CIA, FBI, IRS, BAR –control everything via the 14th Amendment Citizen those who contract to become U.S. citizens as opposed to remaining Sovereign Americans.

If you would like more information on this subject or to understand the code definitions and the language see "Black's Law Dictionary, 5th Ed.", you must decide to not accept the appearances, and false personalities of others, promote honest.

Enough of the government and those who keep our society in slavery by false representation of what and who they really are there are so much to learn about the powers that be.

Think about the real problems, from the information one can only see the minds of those ones who believe it's okay to genocide and secure only for mutual advantages, with belief that part of the United States citizens are but nothing more than freed slaves, aliens from other countries, infants or mentally incompetent, whereby there must be special ones who can control the system of the government in so doing they have graciously step to the plate and accepted the power to control every situation which threaten the one sidedness system of the government of the people to do what they think is best, for whom?

The average person spend most of their time working to serve of self and family results one does not think about the other things that are important, understand able, when there are new challenges each day, holding on to a job today can be a problem when all the large companies are moving out of the country to get lower wage workers.

The money/power system is in the hands of those who know how to generate wealth. There is always going to be a separation of people if people do not understand that we all are "one" people with the same hopes and dreams to make a better life for our families and to be happy and free. There is more I can say but I am like you I value my life and

I'm grateful for what I have, and for what I am going to receive, yet think about the things I've said.

Sociological crimes

In our society today the theories are focus on the socialists which force circumstance, gangs, poverty, drugs, and mental illness.

These are some of the conditions which cause criminal activity in the ones who permit their self to become active in the criminal focus stagnation.

Even within some of these groups who focus these minds on hatred and bigotry, have a sense of right and wrong will not permit the liberation of the right to come forth. They feel a sense of loss of power, and unwilling to be seen in the group eyes as being one who right a wrong.

Unfortunately many are defenders of wrong activities, and not seeing themselves as criminals. Whatever the case may be a person is responsible for their own activities.

Thousands of individuals are placed in jail yearly, often it's the lower social status individuals, ones who are unable to cross the social barriers of the ones with wealth in a materialist bases. Not saying all on the lower financial level is unproductive, it's been notice that under educated, minorities and poor whites are punish low-income and the educational system is not making it easy for them to be educated being the high cost of education in most counties today, there are some countries the education is free..

Yes there are situations which the individual themselves must overcome without becoming a criminal in the pressures of the condition. The person must restraint oneself and respect others and not permit others to become ones victim.

There are views which have a tendency to blame the environment stating that a good environment creates responsible and law-baying people and bad environment creates person with criminal minds and ones who generate violence.

If one take the time to research the matter they will fine there is no separation of the communities where there is no crime, it's all mixed up.

There is crime all over white collar and so-call blue collar whatever, it's all crime.

No matter what you label the activity it comes out criminal activity.

All individuals have a choice, doctors, lawyer even the higher places which we call our justice system and the administration of the country government, by not enforcing the law to protect the citizen from the criminal activity.

Think about some the activities, hate groups, unfair employment which limit the number of employee as being a minority or and the number of immigrates, or discriminate as one of a different belief system other then affected by the majority. Then one must see these acts as being criminal intend.

Let's talk about different belief most people are thinking along the lines of religious believe, which most people are hypnotized and enslaved. But there are many who are Spiritual who have journeyed beyond limitations of the influences of the lower level of thinking which teach separation in the different orders or groups or which think their 'err is the true religion.

We see nearly everywhere in our society people being directed by so-call false prophets, and the people accept the illusions of these persons who come to deceit. Let's speak of a criminal case in 2005 about a religious leader, who was a polygamous, I think you know the sect who believes in polygamy. The FBI releases the information in its crime statistics Intelligence report in the spring 2005 release, stating this person who was sentenced to ten (10) years in prison for the acting as an accomplice to rape. He forced a fourteen (14) years old girl a member of his sect to marry and have sex relations with her nineteen (19) year old-cousin.

I Think people need to give it a rest using God as a way to deceit people, every time someone want people to support their desires they use the word God, its time out and people need to stop feeding into others treacherous activity.

Understand you as adults need to take responsibility it's your duty to protect your children, you've been taught to be unselfish and respect the leaders in the churches, without question and to serve other members and you've been taught this church is special over others groups.

The majority of people take others at their word in the different sects because of the thought of them being religious.

Let's move on to the closing of this topic, there are all types of crimes hated, racist, hostility, all types of social injustice which is a betrayer to the pursuing of a harmony society.

Criminal Personality- type

Psychological theories look at different personality types to try to determine if certain behavioral and trait cause some people to commit crimes. There are many theories but no evidence one way or another to the factors, only things known for certain is that the criminal tend to be sadistic, based in power over others and have no attachment to anyone or thing.

One psychologist claims that psychopath have only low levels of empathy or absence of it altogether and are biologically predisposed to antisocial activity, because they have hyper reactive autonomic nervous system. Also many are motivated by primary object, they do not bond. That means they are motivated to do things that heighten their nervous systems, which mean they have no conscience about hurting others.

There are others believe the criminal minded derive from patterns of social behavior that started when a person in childhood erroneous assumption about crime being caused by society, broken homes, alcoholism in parents, television violence and unemployment. There are those who insist that the criminal minded is vastly different from the responsible people and the patterns derived from behavior in childhood. They reject society and prefer to be criminals.

There are mixed theories, most mental health professions find it difficult to ignore the neurological factors that lead to crimes, certain situations which seem to bring criminal activity, persons with character disorders such as antisocial personality disorder are more prone to acting out aggressively. There are five categories which motivate and influence intoxication for crime, social, situational, impulsive, Cataclysm and compulsive.

Now these categories most people are familiar as for social a certain group having the largest influence is the social environment, the situation could be a stressful circumstances, impulsive sometimes psychotic etc., Cataclysm behavior urge to carry an idea through to a violent act, and sudden explosive act from buildup of tension, and for compulsive part of one's character disorder or fantasy obsession.

Take the person with the split mind (personality), one may think the person is acting because they are in different situations, groups or circles at the time, but in reality they feel inadequacy, people have come to be accustoming to this type characteristic. By it being one percent of the world's population have the illness of Schizophrenia, and so many other people are broad line schizophrenic. The illness age ranges from childhood to late middle age life, but the psychosis is most frequent in adolescence or early adult life.

Researchers believe and suggest the causes may come from a chemical or structural abnormality of the brain. Others believe the causes are complications during pregnancy or birth. There has not been a constant or characteristic structural or biochemical change has yet established the condition. One can only assume and sought in the individual's basic personality and the extent or limit of there're adaptive power to the most general accepted concept of today's world.

How can one be certain, if the childhood conditioning-experience, in transpersonal-experience (mental projection), conflicts, persistent but consciously rejected instinctive urges and drives, feelings of insecurity and other troublesome problems and frustrated purposes in combination or another may be consider as potent precipitating forces.

We all have some uncertainty about the quality of life we live we are going to have the rest of our lives, but we live with the uncertainty. We know in this relative world certain things will take place in time.

Can dissatisfaction, discouragement and detachment play a part in many people's lives initial the symptoms of mild feeling of tension, sleep disturbances and loss of interest in things and some experience hallucination? Think about it acute cases of depression beginning in adolescents and in adults often going long periods of time without change no remission for years which can be modifiable by means of psychoanalysis and treatment.

In brief, the focus is on mental disorders which may contribute to the criminal minded individuals.

I chose schizophrenia because it's the most prevalent of the psychotic disorders and the most misunderstood as a split or multiple personality. The objective is to show a general idea of the influence of mental illness can cause spontaneous emotional difficulties and detachment of reality which could lead to criminal activity.

The good thing about the criminal system when criminal behavior is acted and the defend use a mental disorder to justify the act a psychological assessment is made of the individual.

Also, unmentioned in this chapter so far one of the worse crimes Racism and gender crimes, in how treatment of those somewhat different in physical appears to oneself.

A medical correspondent reported a study by one of the psychology professors in one of the universities in this county in which argues the superiority of certain groups of people based on genes. I want you to think about this, all humans have the same make-up in physical-form. We have one DNA in common, the human DNA. We all are filled with life. We die and are full of spirit the only different in each of us is the way one think and reason.

Now on the physical plane it's the color of our skin, eye, and hair texture, whether one is larger or small than others in body size. Whether female or male the body functions are the same, all have a mind with collective unconscious that mind stuff which all can tap into at will being the source of one's ability to reason and think.

The mental power that all humans have can carry us beyond our own three-dimensional space is the highest qualities one can have in being a human being, it is a spiritual thing which can take you into the higher realms which normally one may be unaware.

There is a process which makes the different in how one connects with others, ones conscious mind repeats what ones learns and place in the subconscious part of your mind. If one receives suggestions in a repeated process it's important to remember the subconscious part of the mind it normally follows the conscious part of the mind, but there is a process of repeat rhythm, like a computer stores information, the subconscious stores suggests and if a subject is repeated is can allow the subconscious to have the ability to take the lead role and the subconscious to overrule the consciousness.

Normally the subconscious mind is to help you to remember. The problem is when a repetition of non-constructive ideas and or criticisms is repeated forms a pattern in one's subconscious.

The damage of implanting harmful ideas into the subconscious, if a person do not become aware of the subconscious speaking to their conscious by repeating statement heard becoming endless broken record.

But there is a way to correct the condition the easiest way is to first, recognize the true nature of the damaging thoughts placed in the subconscious by the repeating suggests to ones subconscious, then start rejecting the suggests by reverse affirmations and turn the thought patterns to positive suggests.

The criminal minded person can do the same thing to change their thought pattern knowing continually of the repeated of the non-productive activities will lead only to death.

Psychological manipulation (Human manipulation)

Some of these examples may be distasteful to some people, knowing the truth hurt sometime even to ourselves times. Knowing that we overlook what is being done to us.

The acts of Psychological manipulation usual derived their strength by and using information to confuse, and using falsehood, though information by big companies and corporations trying to sale there produce with repeating request for one to buy their produce. This causes a subliminal level a region of the conscious which has the capacity to receive accepts and record outside stimuli. In some cases it will bypass the conscious mind and go direct into the subconscious without being sorted for review by the conscious- mind. How many times have heard the kids say "I want to stop there" for the fast food joints, subliminal recording from ideas of others. And all the advertisements for different produces come forward into ones mind to act on.

Another, new problem in our society the private's activity, which one loses their private by giving it away by so-call by improvements You may not think so, if you have one of those new systems, where you can control your home, when you away and see everywhere within. Believe it or not you physically are not the only ones who are motor your home think about it, if you can see; the ones in the systems offices can too. You have given your rights away. We have lost most of our rights in regard to our own homes the new government authority the ones who say they are the security of our land they can come in your homes at will and do whatever they please to you... And even kill your animal's break your things do whatever pleasing to you without recourse. Psychological manipulation overlook this new that controls your personal space the hidden enemy which assassinates ones space in the name of so-call security. It's okay for them to come in your home kill you, your dogs and whom ever they please and say we are law scarcity, "We can come in without your permission." Question, are you free? To be what you desire to be or are you living in a world of fear by others lies and telling you, you need this or the other, the National Guard has been doing a very good job for all these years. What is this new group really trying to do, think about it what is the real purpose behind this group?, Now you know that the National Guard has protected all own land entrance all the doorways into this county, so why all these people trying to deceive you with lies about the true purpose? You know there it a story behind it and we know the truth will come out, but until we as truth seeker come in aliment with one interest, to know the truth about every thing in regard to ones own life. Then the real truth will be known. This is only another form of Psychological Manipulation.

Psychological Manipulation has been around for many years, but used in different name it was "Indoctrination," we have been indoctrinated to believe being functional in what we desire is the only thing that a person needs to be successful in life. The average person is unaware of the trickster and tools the manipulator use to get what they desire of you.

One person god is another person demon. Freedom in mind is true freedom, there are those who prefer to be tied down, bound into ones traditional understanding, and appearances, they prefer and is comfortable with the answers that someone else provides.

I myself want my reader to research all that I have found in my finding to make things clear in their own minds.

The person who is free in their mind recognizes their own talents and refinement, by setting out to fine the truth about life and all its wonders. The power to control ones own mind is sometimes hidden and often mysterious, your mind is your personal place and sacred and must not be manipulated by anyone or thing in this life.

The manipulators is in power all around us in the power sets that make laws and social standards, this false energy is in numbers to decide you and want to get you to accept their way of thinking or acting because its what has been done in the presence and past.

One must seek their own personal power, and push those out who think they have the power, only way they can get you, if you give it to them because they are in the acts of manipulation now, but no exploitation will overcome you, because the influence of freedom in your own mind is in control naturally. Now I should say a person can be manipulated if they are given substance (drugs).

You must have faith in one's own inner knowing and research for oneself not dominated by another view-point, but you holding the rein of your inner-knowing to be true as you view the issues and events in your life and your everyday life.

The rules and reasoning of any society are based on their indoctrination or teaching, and most of the traditions are enslaving peoples minds to conform to their way of thinking and acting by the power of psychical manipulation.

Human Manipulation

Dearly beloved of the presence of all people, it's hard for us to get away from the subject of human manipulation in any form it is breeding like wildfire all across this sweet planet earth, which I love and adore all of its life forms, created by the Source of life. I guess you are thinking what do human- manipulation have to do with the general public; well if your views are evil and desires are against society good, and have a collective view -point which enslave others in a mask of deception then they are crimes.

Understand this is not a put-down or belittle of all traditions, many are systemized. The average human- being only have evolved to a level of coextending with each other even in the religious groups, there are individuals who misuse their giving thrust, who are lacking the knowhow to receive that oneness with the Source, so they follow others in their believe about being the only way. Most people in the religious orders do express values and, there are some who are, using religious traditions for their own personal gain and ego needs by emerge into conflicts and wars. We observe both the weak and strength of individuals and those one's one who adept to the situations and say we can't change things.

There is in fact in many groups there are persons deceiving themselves thinking they are not doing wrong, in reality they kill and destroy others by using deception and physical action, which killing's. minds and bodies, Human-Manipulation.

This information is golden it has the power to change the world's evils influence. If enough of us try to change the mind-set of people for the better things will change.

Let's move into other areas the greatest decision placed before us, is to stop being foolish in thinking its okay to feed the demands of ones ego, the social-environment and all the outside influences which touches ones world. It takes commitment to live ones own life for the good. To learn a deeper and greater knowledge and awareness for the benefit of all life as an individual, we must seek understanding and the gravity of the negative activity and situations that are causing people to become blindsided by those which manipulate and use deceptive meets.

From day one the human mind started to accept and be manipulated, when the doctor made you cry in receiving, ones first breath it's the start of being conscious of ones surrounding and surrendering to the human-psychic. So it's being around from day one, so it's nothing new to the human mind or conscious.

The purpose was to expand the mind for growth and for adaptation to create a miraculous child; another slave incapable of true understand.

Many of us look at the situation differently, as one to conform to the system of society programming the human mind by subliminal subjections. In order to control society there must be a plan for is to work, the easy way is by manipulation of the mind, to get people to do whatever they want them to do, to buy things one doesn't want, even to kill without a real reason, to hate and to love it is all in the game that people play to win in the game of life.

Programming is the name of the game usually by getting people to act to others will, not to ones own will, but to form. We scarcely know whom to blame for the situations for anything; the basest passions of persons in general those who adapt to the views of society actual operate under the system of feeling of good and evil, knowing the focusing now-days are using manipulation is the game..

We all know people desire the bases natural things that will make them happy in life; they know within themselves, they may not be conscious of the entire things required they do have a general ideas. I believe people happy and healthy live without a lot of chaos in their lives, and essential for life to run smooth in their lives.

Let's change the subject a little question; why submit to the suggestions of others which can cause you pain and maybe your dearth? The so call legal drugs that the doctors ask you to take for a condition. Which could kill you?

Many people are so trusting and programmed to society of adaptation, it's another form of manipulation in ones mind, looking at the MD behind the names and you think it's okay to let another person to make decides for you being they are doctors they know what' best for you, not always so, some doctors are in the bed with the drug industry, be cautious in what you take in your bodies, you may be placing your life in others hands ones who may destroy you unknowingly.

Some are being hypnosis to the point where adaptation is their life gold, not realizing it's only another form of the human manipulation (programming).

Knowledge of things beyond the norm, it's for your protection and your survival.

In reality all is belief and one receives greater knowledge, learn all you can learn about things related to your life, just open to the truth there will be a reward in your life

Do you know your potential and how blessed you are to be able to think and reason, most of all you being created in the first place, you were not created to be misused so stop the madness control your own destiny.

The future is in our hands to change things, the greatest and advanced in sciences, technical methods and in medical studies and the other advances in different areas of our learning, the ones who are viewed as the strongest ones.

People look to the nations having the power and influence, and with their leadership, controls the people only to a point, there are many who realize they hold the greatest power in their reality the individual hold the power of oneself, but people give the power to these persons of the world-order in these nations.

One must fall out of love for the easy way or where the familiar fails and come into the chance for a true realization of a perspective that is isolated from the world view of illusions, and feel the truth which brings balances.

Society in this day and age are using the vibration – frequencies though radio and television and other forms of communication to manipulate the people's minds, to their own will as an individual, but to enslave them in believe they need others to think for them, and what they need, in reality its for those persons who are doing the manipulation.

Knowing that all things work through vibrations and frequencies, everything is governed by laws and element of the universal activities, which we all should follow.

Everything is given to us though the true Source in life, we only need to seek it from within oneself in a noble way. Be aware of the messages that come to you through the se devices which try to manipulate your minds. Everything will come to you in Divine order in your life when your-will becomes as the will of the Source of life.

There is another way to over come and rid oneself of this human manipulation activity in your life is to start a meditation practice to cancel-out the messages when others try to manipulate you in any form, your true Source will assist you.

On the inner level, ones judgment an image of the first of life's great challenges develops individually. The problem of choice in life is reflection of ones values, because our choices mirror back to us developing the person one wish to become.

Ones choices are made by ones desires rather than by oneself (inner-self). The consequence of chooses are enormous for they affect all levels in ones life. It's not always the choices that are made by the individuals themselves, or who made the choice;

One may not be yet centered or to young to made the decisions for yourself, or the development values, ethics and Self-knowledge through the messes and conflicts which arise from the choices others persons make for you comes to fruition in your life. One must look carefully at the implications of ones choices, rather than being driven blindly in one's life, if you are under-age one must reliance ones control, until one becomes of accruable for your own choices. Human manipulation or psychological are suggestive, it connects with the various thought patterns. The question, what constitutes a difficult, knowing in different, places in the world down through the ages views are different, what's morality in one country or in one specific relation ship places specific can be the reverse in another,. What is deemed, legal in one part of the world is found illegal in another. So all through are patterns of the law's of morality or in moral at the time of the activity.

The manipulator is one who usually abuses others through their advantage over them. They feed off some persons lazy or-mindless to the facts, of the one not being watchful of others suggests.

One must understand there are persons who feed off others it are a job to many it's not always person. There are times we all have tried to manipulate a situation in our life time. Our minds work through the magnetism of suggestion, we must analyze all thoughts to a degree to accept or to reject, if not one may become off balance and become a slave to the collective society and lost your individuality, canceling ones true desire for yourself.

I'm not saying all forms of manipulation is one of undesirable, it is an action in some cases brings enlighten to truth a wonderful unfolding of ones menial plane of the intuitive, which will inspire you to emanate from the once blind-side of one-self.

The power belongs to every one of us. The higher plane of ones mind, will open and by you welcoming the higher plane of ones consciousness although the plane of ones

Intuition is not ones spirit, it is a channel which communicates to us for our good.

To move off the present subject ones intuition is one next in line to ones enfoldment if one permits oneself to open to it.

The Cosmic Knowledge it that which is above ones intuition; It. only comes to the individual when they become confidence to the point of self realized and thrust in one own juryman. The higher power will give and work with your on an insight level in your life and world, all will come clear. So some human manipulation can be" good, "It will restore you as an individual to a higher- place on the level to enrichment in your own person.

In all I have said, I've tire to speak truth and love for all life to be free.

There is a meditation excise one can do to help you overcome some of the insecurity and help deal with the entities (evil ones) which will cause chaos in ones life.

Let your spiritual self do the work call on the Source of life, to amplify your development. Let this exercise become apart of your daily activity ritual, in the morning and or night-time or both times, it will help you to overcome all unwanted thoughts to in bed in ones subconscious as you connect with your Source of life as you enter meditation ones sacred space.

The exercise as follow: Say to yourself, "I am the reflection of my god-part; I was a victim of my lower-self overcome by disturbed by sociality, of the outer contacts.

Now all is open to me for my good, I love my body and mind it is the body and mind of my God, I now have peace within my being. I resolve to love all creations of the Source of life (God) and surrender my will to God will and love." And So It Will Be"

This is a starter WHEN YOU COME TO THE PLACE OF SELF ANALYSIS YOU WILL SEEK OUT MORE FROM SOURCES IN THE WORLD OF ENLIGHTMENT.

Social Hate Crimes

All the hatred from the old programmed society is still around after a half a millennium. The hate groups are on the rise, large groups small groups it seem a non ending battle to overcome hatred and bigotry, of pair, sorry, hatred and the problem being there are people with small minds, trying to find something to make them personally important and special; in their reality we all are special in being human.

People, who speculate and spread rumors that under mind the very creative power of our Source to make a mistake in the development of the humankind is delusional, and we should not be permitting others of evil to teach our young people in shaping their minds.

Many incidents of violence against others are racially motivated crimes. Public record show many cases; let it be known in this article there is no discrimination in regard to race if you are racist and hate exist you fall in one of these groups, it moments not the group being black, red, brown, yellow or white, if your group intend is to do harm of violence or deception into hatred of another person because of the color of their skin or religious opinion believer's it's still a crime to harm others.

There are people who deceit their selves in appearances and in one thing words, if you really listen to what people say, like "you people, pigs, white devils, niggers, etc., a serious doubt will arise which supports the popular opinion that the civil rights movement of the 60's has made a different in the way people really feel about others.

Let's take a look at some of the cases since the civil rights act of the 1960's; a report published showing the racist tension that was on the rise.

We have many people in this county who are racial motivated they spew out hate for others who look different and think different. The most highlighted are the ones that have been around for sometime like the ones who cover their heads with sheets to conceal their identity and the other group removes their hair to show other they are in a group who show and spread hate and social unjustly movements, these groups are coming together joining their powers in the campaign to stop us from being a united people.

There are bigots in high places, in government and business corporations, also the new media, which gives only half-true's, many companies who are undercover in their politicians and views about people.

But these people have influenced on people who are weak and those lacking in knowledge on certain subject matter, these are ones who are vulnerable and are willing to aspect what is took to them.

We have persons in our learning institutes who are racist, others who represent all of us in government who make decisions in regards to peoples lives. Some of the news media have some under cover issues about racist some editors and journalist even now and then will slip –up and say or write something that tells the real story about them personally.

People need to understand what goes around come around, maybe not in this life or the next but all activity one create in one's life has a result and one must face that result.

When a person feels inferior they try to belittle others, the can it is they fear. By not understanding those same persons may become their benefactor. We all have something contribute to society whether to improve or the opposite.

Many thoughts are based on where the different groups originated from and their cultural background would detect how they live their lives, yes this can be a problem if the people lack cultural refinement. Many see Africa as primarily of the jungle group unrefined, living in poverty and mud houses and they see Latino's as slave labor struggling for a place in society.

Many are undercover in regards to their views on racism, because they are racists themselves and some these persons are candidates for political achievement and are campaigning for the highest offices in government has to offer to a person, if those persons get in those positions to control the people are in trouble.

There is one more thing on this subject, think about the neo-Nazis (Hitler) movement in the 40's some of these persons supporting Hitler's ideas now are the same persons fight during World War II against Hitler's ideas, and you know there are some men with collars turn around so-call ministries of god (notice the small "g") are performing the "hail Hitler" and make statements implicating blacks are soulless mud people, this statement was make by a so-call pastor of a church.

Understand these people are so very ignorant and blinded by hate they would not understand the truth about creation then the mud under their own feet; this was a person of the sheet cover group. Is not intelligence enough to understand the Source of life do not creates anything imperfect being the supreme God we know do not indignity or enforce bigotry? What sense does that make to you?

As for those sheet cover group movement and the Anti- radical traditionalist movements called the societies, of X and Nazi though group are now joining forces with the idea promoting hatred and anti-human views.

The focus is global spread of hatred, its deadly, the majority of these hate groups have members with personality disorders and they have lack of remorse in their activities, which cause harm to others and in their acts in disregard for others, they are preoccupy with the belief other peoples ambition for a better life will interfere with the quality of their lives.

The psychological traits are more likely to generate the acts of crimes, crimes of exploiting others, and insist that their way of thinking vastly better than others to the point of unsafe activity and disregard for oneself and others within the group.

As for their children you will generally see signs of behavior problems. Reason being the children is not permitted choices but forced to accept the views of their social environment and families. The influence is so great they may not recover from the powers that be. In turn they lose all sense of self-importance to develop normally to be in the surround human societies.

The rigid patterns of hatred have destructed their deserving ideal of love for their fellowman. The potentiality for meeting and learn about others views and supports of teachers outside of the groups is merely a dream if the children are not released from the evil learning vehicles of hatred and bigotry.

As the moments materialize apparent flashes of answers slowly as we utter but have failure to this time of the mental demand upon the subconscious mind is not voiced in words of the apparent damage and danger of this continuous activity.

The process of character building should not be in hands of hate groups or the ones who delight in destruction, perhaps these groups are weak who allows themselves to be made by others weak ones. True strong character is build by strong ones of moral and ethics.

We are taught to make mental picture of our desired conditions, if we say I dislike or hate that person because he's black or white, or others, rich or poor the sense of loss will be felt in you. Not understanding those particular persons just may assist you in your life's needs.

All human life is special; in fact all life serves its purpose in their quest of existence. Mankind is the product of three principal lines of evolution not to get confuse with some of the erroneous ideas of Darwinian evolution the different is the spiritual process.

In reality humans are classify into seven main principles to be in harmony with great natural laws as in the division of light, sound and the chemical elements etc.

Humans are arranged in the major divisions for convenience, the three components are spirit, soul and body. Not to get off the main subject will be brief.

The average person desire is limited as a rule to the narrow personal interest. Therefore if the person is not unfolding, only accepting the deceptive views and there activity then there will not be higher qualities to show of the positive and upper discovers outside the fixed dominant provisions of their negative tendencies.

The higher qualities which shows compassion and morality can only come when a person decides to evolve to a higher level where the motivation is no longer in the form of hatred and bogey which shows ones under degeneration which causes a criminal minded person.

Unfortunately, due to ignorance and the unknown self-hate the person like so many are often using their power over the weak minded ones to secure their own need to feel higher regardless of the rights and welfare of others.

We as humans cannot find anything more fundamental than our own conscious existence and the use of that consciousness analogy our activities whether good or evil.

Humankind is a product of the Cosmic Creation with the spark of the Divine principals in evolvement, but there is a gap even in the enfoldment of ones self-consciousness of who you really are as a human-being.

Unfortunately the criminal-minded person have not evolved enough to realize to create disharmony between individuals comes with an appetite that builds the wrong karma and the taste will not be to your liking, there is a result in the action of each one of us, and if we create wrong causes wrong results will come. Mostly, in the form of suffering of some type, frequently they come in physical or mental diseases.

Not saying there isn't a mental disorder present now, most of the time there is a mental disorder in the beginning. But creating non-productive karma with some type of mental disorder does not make you exempt from the non-productive results of the law of cause and effect. The law of cause and effect works for all creations.

This being a moral and ethical universe it has its rules and laws of order and these laws are disregarded by the criminal minded persons which in time will receive the return of their actions in a form of learn though mostly suffering of the same type or maybe not in this lifetime, but future life time because the actions must in turn be learn by the ones who enforced this type of creation. Whatever one does there is a lesion to be learn either now or later the lessons will be learns.

The criminal minded of whom I am referring has confounded their thinking to the sinister forces as one may think in the form of the religious theories explains "sinner."

As most criminal minded persons instead of looking within themselves, they accuse others for their down fall, not accepting responsibility for their own acts. Misunderstanding when one reach the age in decision making it's your responsibility to make the right decisions for oneself.

As some who try to justify or defend their acts in wrong doing some produce the illusion in their own minds that God orchestrated the plan, and the end results sums up to blaming his creator for all the wrong in their lives

The criminal in their evilness refuse to believe their own personal ego consciously allies itself with the evil forces in their lower-self resulting in serious under-growth in character and as it persist will end finally in the annihilation of the persons physical and mental existence

Fortunately the moment minds are awakened a choice is made in the direction the person will fashion their lives, the intellect or knowledge of right and wrong with ones free will to chose whatever direction they desire brings the end results.

The question must be ask and answered, why would anyone should desire to act contrary to the moral laws in place?

Primarily it's due to ignorance of the comeback consequents also as being persons of undeveloped state which are influence with wrong teaching. The average criminal does not clearly perceive their actions as immoral or against the moral laws. He lives within his own personality. Until the complexities of the criminal nature actually begin to unravel and the process for ones enfoldment to filters down to activate the hidden treasures of one's true purpose and the desires of the universe given over to ones lower-self to dominate the mind and personality, by the higher-self or spiritual illumination that which has been diseased with evilness.

The secret to opening this mystical door for renewal is the cosmic key within ones cells of one's brain and it's the reprogramming of the subconscious memories or mind that has branched out from old programming of the negative characteristics of the activities and habits of the past.

Perhaps since birth one may have been programmed wrongly by others, and even their own family members, it can be also by the educational system, and knowing there are many systems, television, and new media, associates and ones peers there are those who are well trained in deception, which can make one development into an inferior or, weak and unhappy person to act in violence toward others and themselves in the process of all their activities.

There is a form of reprogramming is to open the mind of an individual to receive the true meaning of life, will give one pride within their selves to attract a quality personality which will magnetize improvement for a valuable character.

Are different types of form of deception being acted in doing business, contracts are the main problems, the use in wording that deceit or mislead people.

There is all type of so call Consumers Protection groups, but, are they truly effective for its needs? Contracts are an agreement made between different parties. In that contract it should be explain the nature of valid, void, violability and unenforceable contracts. This means that all parties know the terms and all parties must have a legal recognized interest in the subject of the contract.

The Governing Houses Gangsters (govt. officials)

It's a sad day, knowing the ones whom we trust to care for our interest in this country turn out to be in the bed with our oppressors and being a part of our problems here in American.

I am talking about the law-makers who permit big industries and corporations in this country to be the source of the exploitation of its citizens and; this is not speculation, but a real plot to keep the American people in crisis.

The truth is coming out now through the voices of people with concerns for the citizens of American. The government agencies have laws and codes in which they follow, but who make these laws and codes? The same ones, the government do, every law and code is outlined by persons in the government agencies to conform to their (government) interest.

Many of the private companies have bought their way into the good graces of many of the government official by way of individual's personal gifts. Those who want these gifts from the big companies are those who sole their loyalty to the companies for self gain. Ones, who work for government who create laws which govern the peoples gain or loses, Companies like Banks, credit cards companies, mortgage companies, etc., and you can say, all those who are lenders, also the utility companies, if they were able they would try to sell you the Air we breath and the light that comes from the Sun.

Do not forget the Food companies, people are confuse by all the different labels on the meats, and vegetables, not knowing what is save or best buy because of the health risk; We know many of this disclosures will cause people to look at these companies a little-harder, think about the Bankers and or mortgage companies and credit card companies in different light because some are receiving gifts, for their future or gifts of money changing hands as contributing to some of the officials, projects they receive by different ways from these companies.

Have you notice if a utility company want a rate increase no problem, they go to the utility commissioners(govt., official) who decide if or should they get the increase, most of the time it's approved. We are not responsible for their equipment, or electrical system, taxes or repair or their expansion. If they would upgrade their service by placing the lines under-ground when the severe storms and hurricane come it would be less chance of outages, and less chance of electrical-energy in the atmosphere They put up large power lines, which feed the small ones in areas, where there are populated, knowing the energy in the high populated areas could cause cancer. They place them in areas like schools, apartment buildings, houses etc. They get what they want ever time, what can I say. The financial giants around the globe are in control even the government does not have enough power because it's divided in its members to over- turn the ultimate betrayal of the people, because their hearts are filled with personal greed, they have the final say by their decision.

The manipulation of some politician with their words of deceit are enslaving continuously, when a man is sick he feel justified in taking medication he thinks will heal him, so it is with a politician he uses words that will satisfy the people but do not deliver. If the people try to rebel against the actions of the ones who place them in harm-way than the people are shown as wrong for reacting, but in reality the one used deceit, they should be called the unlawful ones. But are the people justify in their agitation against the appalling activity of the officials and the companies?

Think about this, before each meeting on the Hill, there is a tradition excises a minister come and pray over the meetings for good things to come out of the meeting. It's hard to think what these people are thinking; they are fantasizing because many are not concern about noble activity only about personal gain, egotism, self-gratification and just having power to say "no" to situation that will assist the needs of the average citizen, not companies which take the jobs out of the country, so their company executives can take to the air in their own private Jets, and live on expense accounts, and pocket their millions of dollar income without taxation..

As for the educational systems our young people are enslaved by loans for their life –time paying off the loans, which the country should be giving to our children free. Other countries educate their children free what's with that picture?

In this country people believe there is an American dream, but is this dream for the people or for the large corporations, believes its okay to bleed the people as long as the governing, body's officials let these companies do so.

What can I say, we put those people in the position they are in. We need to take back the country, meaning those who believe in justice for all in using uprightness and honor in regard to the needs of the people in this country.

Each person who in their evil doing is living in a world of make-believe, ones action will come-up again, remember the law of cause and effect, it will return.

Just think a moment, putting your-self in the place of the victims. Use this illustration: Its only through examination or experience that one can really understand the gravity of a situation, and the process to comprehend anything of the human sense until touches oneself, think about this, it is only by loving that one understand love, and being that love which you comprehends, and no longer speculate. Another example, as you looks at a flower and see its beauty or smell the fragrance a feeling of enjoyment overtake you because your observing beauty in that moment you temporarily become the flower, understanding all the flower means to itself and in itself.

The same is when one comes to the point of not merely talking about a situation but consciously grasping the situation personally. It become clear enough from the very thought that there is really no getting around making a change in ones conscious and start on to the pathway to one's own truth, that means all of us have a part of truth within them.

The path of reality and truth is within one's own heart, one must first step on the path moving in the direction for change for the better.

We human live in a marvelous world, the discoveries are endless and we are in process of discoveries the concept of universal love and how to respect and love life.

The Breathless Breast-man-
Crimes against other forms of life

Let me examine or explain what a human really is; one with a mind, heart, and soul of love. But a breast-man is one who illusory his own- self in thinking he is human. Why, because he has all the make-up as a human-being in physical- form, but not the true essence.

"The smallest pebble wafers and disturbs the clam waters. Every effect of a cause are never limited to the boundaries of the cause, nor can the results of the crime be confined to the pebbles, which may be small and not visible on the surface, but below the pebbles are building up and forcing the water to be moved in a different direction, no longer to be able to keep it's natural course. The beast-man is blind to his criminal activities because he is against life on the planet.

Other life forms are being push out of their original home areas, which gave them safety and peaceful living. The breath-man is totally blind to the needs of other forms of life. He sees only the wealth of the land, and not being one with a watchful eye of the welfare of the inheritances of the land.

There are stories of all types of crimes against other forms of life for the purpose of gain its cover-up with the so-call thought of progress. What person in their right mind would think using earth-movers to up-root trees, to build a parking lot for cars for a Shopping- Centers as progress; do you think its progress! Removal of trees which gives life on the planet, one which preventable of diseases, medical alder, trees and plants give fruits and herbs in the form of fertilize and nourishment for the bodies of all life on the planet.

For a start, let speak in general, of the woodland or the forests its beautiful trees of different colors and shapes high and lows, the old trees stand 150 ft., or more in the height and has lived 300 to 400 years. If they are not cut down to make way for so-call improvements for man's comfort or accommodation. As the trees grow they respect each other by standing well apart, as if intolerant of each other's shadow even the trees know their needs for full sunlight in it time. They seem to fine their place to meet their special requirements to serve like soil, slopes, drainage, temperature, rainfall and other conditions. They make no choices, letting their seeds fall at will wherever the need are and for whatever purpose of that location it's meet accord to the plan of life

There are plants everywhere from the beautiful rainforests to the dry desert all on a calm summer day stand motionless and silent. They seem to know what is required of them, but seem to be concord about the activity around them. They seem to be enter-wine with their purpose for it's working within them is a tremendous activity at work for their survival and growth. The water and nutritious are being drawn from the soil by their roots, and gases are accede from the air by their leaves. At the same time the leaves capturing the energy of sunlight that is releasing it in the forests s special compound energy food from over 93 million star miles away to feed the plants. Do not forget about the animals that eat the leaves or plants from the trees in the forests, like the Deer's wandering along cropping the leaves, the wild turkeys flock in the Oaks and Pine to gorge themselves on acorns and nuts.

Let's think about those wonder Rainforests, around the world which house many species of life. Note this; the tropical rainforests has been called the jewels of the earth and the world's largest pharmacy because of the national medicines has been discovered in those areas.

The deforestation, biologists have estimated that large numbers of species on earth are being driven to extinction and exterminated within 50 years by the breast-man in his greed for so-call progress or his ego it's all a "lie," deceit has been around since relative-time begin. People lie for no reason, so it became a habit to lie, and to them it's right, because that what makes them happy. In reality it's a need to control the destiny of life forms on the planet. Almost 90% (percent) of the West-Africa's Rainforest has been destroyed. Estimated deforestation of the Amazon Rainforest could be wipe-out by 2030 and Madagascar has lost 60% do to illegal logging.

These and other forests are homes to a number of species of life on this planet, animals and vegetation all of which are a must to the balance of life on the planet.

Why people are so easily approve of what is recommend by others who have no vision or knowledge about anything? Tell me, why people are so willing to destroy the future of life on this planet by being a blind follower of ignorance's?

There forests produce Oxygen which all life need on earth and I ask you what will happen if we do not have air, all I can see is the lost of our resources for survival, and the breast-man see personal-gain in the form of power over something and dollars-signs.

Let's look at the problem facing all life forms by "Genetically Engineering," though and by large corporations and chemistry laboratories in their alteration of the species DNA. These corporations who have an interest in making more money by this journey, Bio-Tech for example, take the trees the lumber companies are changing the original make-up of many trees by BT a toxin in the root systems of many trees causing other form of life to die, what means the poison chemistry destroy other life like the ones who eat the leafs on the trees, and there are many who eat the fruits' of trees.

Not understanding or care about the after-math of their alteration of the created species. All life creatures have specific purpose in their make-up, it's not our job or right to change that purpose, it only creates inadequate to its nature.

Mankind thinks he is beyond the law of accountability for their actions, there come a price one pay for their egotistical arrogant towards life. If you like to know more about Genetically Engineered species feel free to research it for your self. A good place to start is Ecology to see the effects it has on the environment.

The realization of the knowing what is right and what is wrong with the minds of the so-call human is in the activity which destroys other life forms

Let, focus on the life forms that live in the so-call wild those areas we only visit from time to time and separate ourselves from by highways and shopping malls, parking lot etc. There are reasons why the majority of humanity is ignorance and out of touché with the needs of other forms of life, it's because one do not see them as important.

Now I will example some things about the different species who life in nature beautiful spaces, first understand we all came from the same matter, all energy and atoms etc., we started at the pattern on our own design. All in contemplation of a life of mystery unknown to us as we were formed though the sacred circle of life to behold vastness of the universe. All of us in our own forms are hoping life will be sweet for the asking faithfully thanking our True Source for all the good that is given to us. Now let's move to the species living in the areas which seem to upset people because they cannot accept that they are the intruders in others space.

The first one is the Deer there is medicine- power in Deer's that power is gentleness, since the deer is the so-call problem child for people that has become the invasions of the Deer space. Understand, one must see the Deer's side, see the Deer seeking food where there is none, because it's been removed by people who want more space, so they displace the original owners out of their home the deer and people have the nerve to feel displeasure about the Deer come to a place out of habit that once gave them food, water and assure them from harm. Hard to believe that people are so uneducated about other forms of life they believe they are right in their actions to destroy what is not their right, and to know what they want is to destroy the Deer's because they displease with them.

The Deer live in a variety of biomes ranging from tundra to the tropical rainforest. While often associated with forests, many deer are acetones species that live in the transitional areas between forests and thickets (for cover) and prairie and savanna (open space). The small species of brocket Deer and Purus of Central and South America and Muntjacs of Asia generally occupy dense forests and less often seen eye open spaces, with the exception of the Manta of Indian. Now the highest concentration of large Deer species is in the temperate North America lies in the Canadian Rocky Mountain and Columbia Mountain Regions between Alberta and British Columbia where all five North American deer species (White - tailed deer, Mule deer, Caribou, Elk, and Moose) can be found. Australia has six species there are fallow deer, Red Deer, Sabar Deer, hog Deer, Rusa Deer, and Chital.

Biology the Deer is an excellent jumper and swimmer, their legs are powerful suited for rugged woodland terrain, generally they have lithe, compact bodies. Deer are also have four-chambered stomach, their teeth are adapted to feeding on vegetation and other ruminants, they lack upper incisor, instead have a tough pad at the front of their upper jaw. As for their food, deer are selective feeders, they usually brewers, primarily feed on leaves, because their stomachs are small high nutrient is required than attempt to digest vast quantities of low-grade, fibrous food. The deer select easily digestible shoots, young leaves, fresh grasses, soft twigs, fruit, fungi, and lichens.

As for a doe generally has one or two fawns at a time, the gestation period is anywhere up to 10 months for the European Roe Deer, most fawns are born with their fur covered with white spots; many species lose their spots once they get older. In the first twenty minutes of a fawn's life, the fawn begins to take its first steps. That's something to think about we humans it takes 6 months to a year. There much more I could say but there is another area I would like to speak on.

This will be in form of partly a story, in showing how we as humans can learn from this beautiful creature; One day fawn heard a voice from Great Spirit from the Sacred Mountain. fawn immediately started up the trail to meet with Great Spirit because she knew she was going to connect with the Source of all good, knowing it was only love that would be given her, as she became nearer dreaming of the fresh sweet leaves of yesterday rain and moving of the clear water over the hill waiting for her to receive, closer she heard something on the trail, as she looked up there was horrible demon blocking her pathway to Great Spirit. The demon was trying to keep all the creations from connecting with the good from Great Spirit gifts of love send from above. Fawn gently, said with so much love filled her heart, please let me pass, but the demon said no matter how you ask I will not let you pass to receive Great Spirit gifts.

In saying this in the story, we humans forget that all life have the same needs as each other, all is life one must respect life in all forms. The Deer is so gentle and loving how one not see and feel the love, they are like a flower of kindness, and they embrace goodness from afar.

Let's move to the next one the Fox, which is known for his medicine power in the form of camouflage and is a common name for many species of carnivorous mammals belonging to the Canines family. There are 37 species referred to as foxes, of which only 12 species actually belong to the Vulpes genus of true foxes. Unlike many candies, fox are not usually pack animals. Typically they live in small family groups, opportunistic feeders that hunt live prey 9especially rodents). Foxes also gather a wide variety of other foods ranging from grasshoppers to fruit and berries. The diet of the fox is largely made up of invertebrates however it also includes rabbits, and other small mammals, reptiles, - (snakes), amphibians, grasses, fruit, fish, birds, eggs, dung beetles and all kind of small animals.

The Fox is extremely wary of humans, fox attack on humans are not common.

In the wild foxes can live for up to 10 years, but most foxes only live for 2 to 3 years due to hunting, road accidents and diseases.

Fox hunting is a controversial sport that originated in the United Kingdom in the 16th century. One good thing is that hunting with dogs is now banned in the United Kingdom though hunting without dogs is still permitted. The so-call sport is practiced in several other counties including Australia, Canada, France, Ireland, Italy, Russia and the United States.

Now the story goes like this; Mr. fox said to himself I must vanish amidst the lush undergrowth of the forest for gives me protection from the predators call man who hunts me for my tail as a form of sport, knowing I would die from bleeding from the lost of my tail, they release the dogs on me to yank my flash from my soul, and eating me while *I am* still alive. The Fox only dream of when his ability was to meld into ones surroundings and be unnoticed though the powerful gift of love given to him, once observed the hunter unnoticed. "Fox where are you, under the ferns or are you becoming the forest, can you blend in now your snow coved hill, Oh no the blood is red that comes from my wounds leaving me open unprotected, now all is just a game to the predator-man."

The next is a symbol of sacredness of every walk of life, telling us to reconnect to the true meaning of life. All animals are sacred, but I want to speak of the Bison (Buffalo) in the tradition of many Native Americans people the White Buffalo is the most sacred, the appearance of White buffalo is a sign that prayers are being heard, that the promises of prophesy are being fulfilled. White buffalo signals a time of change and abundance.

The Bison were hunted almost to extinction in the 16th century and were reduced to a few hundred by the mid-1880s. They were hunted for their skins, with the rest of the parties of the animal left behind to decay on the ground. After the animals rotted, their bones were collected and shipped back east in large quantities. The US Army sanctioned actively endorsed the wholesale slaughter of Bison herds. The US Federal government promoted bison hunting for from other bovines, and primarily to weaken the North American Indian population by removing their main food source and to pressure them onto the reservations. Knowing without the Buffalo, native people of the plains were forced to leave the land or starve to death.

According to historian Pokka Hamalainen, Native Americans also contributed to the collapse of the bison. By the 1830s the Comanche and the allies on the Southern plains were killing about 280,000 bison a year. By, 1845 and lasting into 1860s, which caused a widespread of collapse of the bison herds. In 1860s the rains came which helped the herds to somewhat recover to a degree.

The railroad industry also had a hand in eliminating of the bison herds, reason being they wanted bison culled the herds of bison being on the tracks and believed they could cause damage and the bison took shelter in cuts though mountain and hill in the time of high winds and harsh winter condition by the bison eking these areas it delay trains for days, so the predator-man killed the herds using commercial hunting the skins were used for industrial machine belts, clothing etc., The commercial enterprise, involving organized teams of professional hunters. The hunter would customarily locate the herd in the early morning and station himself, shooting the animal's broadside through the lungs. The bison would drop. Many of these professional hunters, such as Buffalo Bill Cody killed over a hundred animals at a single stand and many of those professional hunters killed over a thousand in their career, and one professional hunter killed over 20,000 by his own count. For a decade from 1873 there was several hundred, perhaps over a thousand, commercial hide hunting outfits harvesting bison at any one time. The commercial take arguably was anywhere from 2,000 to 100,000, animals per day depending on the season.

In 1874, President Ulysses S. Grant voted a Federal bill to protect the dwindling bison herds. In 1875 General Philip Sheridan pleaded to joint session of congress to slaughter the herds to deprive the Indians of their source of food. By 1884, the American bison was close to extinction.

The only continuously wild bison herd in the United State resides within Yellowstone National Park. Numbering between 3,000 and 3,500 this herd is survived the mass slaughter of the 1800s by hiding out in the pelican Valley of Yellowstone Park.

Now after hearing all of this, I would like you to think about how would you feel if your life was in chaos every moment and your family was being slaughter in front your eyes?

There is magic or medicine in the Buffalo, the Buffalo is a symbol of sacrifice and service to all, perhaps one can say the buffalo (people) agreed to give their lives so the America Indian could have food for themselves and children and shelter from cold winters and summer heat and clothing to protect their skin. The Buffalo represents a manifestation of sacrifice thought in the divine aspect of life in all that is of goodness.

Next, let's speak of the Cougar known as the mountain lion, panther, or catamount, depending on the region. This large, solitary cat has any wild terrestrial mammal in the Western hemisphere, extending from Yukon in Canada to the Southern Andes of South America.

The Cougar is a predator it will stalk and ambush its prey, it has variety food sources to choose such as deer, elk, big-sheep and some domestic animals like cattle, horses, sheep, particularly in the northern part of its range, but it also hunts species as small as insects and rodents. The Cougar are always in competition with other like predator like the Jaguar, Gray Wolf, Grizzly Bear, and the American Black Bear for food.

The Cougar is the largest of the small cats, the cougar it known for its leadership ability it is placed in the subfamily Felines.

Though capable of sprinting, the cougar is typically an ambush predator, it stalks through brush's and trees, across, ledges, or other covered spots, before delivering a powerful leap onto the back of its prey with a strong bite to the neck.

Like almost all cats, the Cougar is a solitary animal. Their social structure is like most, only the mother and kittens live in groups, when they become adults they separates and the males meet with the female only to mate. The life expectancy in the wild is between8 to 13 years, and probably averages 8 to 10; a female of at least 18 years, cougars may live as long 20 years in captivity.

The World Conservation Union (IUCN) currently lists the cougar as a "least concern" species. The Cougar is regulated under Appendix I of the Convention on International Trade in Endangered Species of Wild Fauna and Flora (CITES), rendering illegal international trade in specimens or parts. In the year of 1996, Cougar hunting was prohibited in Argentina, Brazil, Bolivia, Chile, Colombia, Costa Rica, French Guiana, Guiana, Guatemala, Honduras, Nicaragua, Panama, Paraguay, Suriname, Venezuela, and Uruguay. (Costa and Panama) Cougar still are unprotected in El Salvador, and Guyana, although legal protection is place for Cougar in some counties there is continuous killing of this animal in the United States and Canada. It is permitted in every U.S. state from the Rocky Mountains to the Pacific Ocean, with the exception of California. Cougars are generally hunted with packs of dogs, until the animal is treed. When the hunter arrives on the scene, he shoots the cougar from the tree at close range.

Due to the expanding human population, cougar ranges increasingly overlap with areas inhabited by humans. It's a rarity that Cougars attack humans, the Cougar do not recognizes humans as prey it's a learning behavior and if attack occur it's in the spring and summer when juveniles cougars leave their mothers it's in a condition of severe starvation and search for new territory, or if they are cornered.

The grace and power f the cougar have been widely admired in the cultures of the indigenous people of Americas. The Inca city of Cusco is reported to have been designed in the shape of a cougar, and the animal also gave it name to both Inca regions and the people. The Mocha people represented the puma often in their ceramics. The sky and thunder god of the Inca, Viracocha, has been associated with the cougar.

The cougar spirit represents power, grace and stealth in darkness, but its real power lies in the silence of its eerie unblinking stare that seems to bore deep into one's soul. This teaching can help us to discover the benefits of concentration, deep contemplation and prayer. As we peer into the darkness of the unknown we feel its power, as the cougar we wait for the movement in the field of darkness and let spirit guide us through just as the cougar friend does, we to come to the light on the other side away from the darkness which tried to hold us from the light.

Moving on to the next the Beaver as expect master builder and their talents are many and simple because most qualities of the beaver can be emulated by humans. For one they can show us humans how to be in harmony with nature and ones environment.

These creature is excellent swimmers, with the ability to holds its breath under water for along time. As a water creature the beaver spirit is deep within where dreams past and knowledge begin in the subconscious store-house of our mind.

The beaver are very industrious, hard workers and are tenacious in whatever project they undertake. The beaver large teeth are among its most prized possessions and they continue to grow until the moment of death. This shows us that the Source of life only creates excellence in all life- forms (creatures), at the teeth of this beautiful animal, we humans lose a tooth that's it. And as for its fur it's highly prized because it is both soft and waterproof.

The Beaver spirit is never defeated they have a gentle nature, makes friends with other creatures easily who are in their domain. The Beaver can show us humans and be a reminder that we are the master architects of our own lives and as we alter our lives we alter our environment and world. Beaver is the doer one of the animal kingdom and as for its medicine is akin to water and earth energy, and incorporate a strong sense of family and home. If you were to look at the dams that block the woodland streams you would find several entrances and exits, why because they are wise they will not leave themselves open without alternative escape routes in time of danger. In regards to those teeth which capable of felling whole trees, although the beaver is friendly imagine if a predator come to attack what those teeth can do they and from the rear, the beaver is armed with paddle tail that aids in swimming as well as in guarding it's behind. As for the insight to its medicine or wisdom I must look beyond architect and see the wisdom, the power of working and attaining a sense of achievement in building one dream to accomplish ones goal. They are telling us to look for alternative solutions to our life's challenges and to protect the creations of life all around you in the form of natures gifts and put real love and energy into whatever your heart desire, along with being watchful of false appearances.

Next is the Bear, which shows introspection, is found on every continent and comes in many sizes and colors. The bear is revered on every continent especially North America where there are people who believe the Bear was once human and has great mystery in their lives of the spirit of the bear. Many American Indian tribes have bear clans and perform ceremonies in regard to the bear. Many believe in bear medicine as being powerful and they also bears are guides to the river of meaning.

There are those who are ignorance to the true understanding or it translation of the medicine and or power, people are starting to kill bears for their clans to improve or so-call enhances their sexual ability, to take a life for a moment of gratification which is not real it's an illusion, people want to believe something to be true, so a thought is placed in the mind and they receive it, just lies the small minded blind followers they always have been, believing what others say to be true, without thinking about the results to other form of life, for that one moment of gratification which is a lie in the first place, all sexual desire comes from one's mind.

Reports of Bear killing in the national parks and other mountain and forests, are on the rise because of the ignorance of people who are letting their physical wants destroy life.

The bear is a solitary dweller and a master of his domain; he is a teacher to mankind in the form of being humane and the importance of being an independent thinker and to seek peace with all life.

The bear is the embodiment of strength and is fierce to a threat on its lair, it is not wise to come between the mother bear and her cubs, teaching us ways to always protest those we love, and how much more we are to protect all life forms for their divine-purpose on mother earth. There are not here to feed us with their fresh or clans.

Many times people have avoided the knowledge of others forms of life purpose because they do not know their own purpose in life. The bear knows the great void is the place where all solutions and answers live in harmony with the questions that fill our true realities. We must also believe that the answers to all questions reside within us. Each and every being has the capacity to quiet their mind, and enter the silence and know whatever is needed at the time and it has nothing to do with destroying of life.

In India, the cave symbolizes the cave of Brahma. Brahma's cave is considered to be the pineal gland that sits in the center of the four lobes of the brain. Bears, seeks honey, or the sweetness of truth, within the hollow of old trees, if the trees are destroyed where can he get the sweetness? In the winter, when mother earth sleeps from the labor of summer to reinsure with its Source the bear enter the womb-cave to hibernate, as the winter assist in digesting the year's life experiences. It has been said that our goals reside in the consciousness, and to accomplish ones goals and dreams that we must carry and develop the art of introspection.

Next is the Armadillo, who is one that understands the necessity of spiritual purification and love, but knows the need for his armor that he wears on its back. The Armadillo boundaries of safety are a part of it total being, armadillos roll into a ball and never be penetrated by enemies. The gift from the Armadillo is the lesson for one to set boundaries in all areas in life. These boundaries become a shield that wards off things which are undesirable to you. The shield reflects what you are and what your will accept from others on an unconscious level. This will set up boundaries that allow only chosen experiences to be a part of your life. Outside of the shield one may put whatever one is willing to experience by invitation only.

The key to the joy in life is to be like the Armadillo wisdom, his underside is soft, but its armor will protect the softness if the boundaries are in place.

The Butterfly a bringer of joy and peace, as they cultures all over earth revere its delicate and colorful beauty, although they only live for a week or two, with the exception of the Angle wing and Monarch live about six months.

The butterfly represents the process of transformation and shape shifting. When you see a butterfly coming toward you think of issues confronting you and what state of mind or change are you in regards to the situation facing you... The butterfly is symbolic of early spiritual growth, and brings to us is akin to the air it is the mind, and the ability to know the mind or to change it. It is the art of transformation. To use the lesson you must astutely observe your position in the cycle of self-transformation, in doing so think of the Butterfly in its experiences three stages of development from being in a cocoon to caterpillar to an adult butterfly. Think about the stages we humans are subject to the body, mind and soul; these three things are the relative changes of the human evolvement, where as the Spirit is the Divine aspiring of the Universe. The Butterfly in its changes is like our stages of changes forever changing.

Like the Butterfly you are always at a certain station in your life activities, you may be in an egg stage, which is the beginning as womb experience, it's the stage at which an idea is born, but has not yet become a reality. Next the larva stage is the point in which one decides to create the ideal starting point for the idea hoping the parts will together without physical action performed in the world. Next the cocoon stage involves going within doing or developing and projecting idea which will become your ideal personality. Finally full stage of one's transformation in ones leaving the chrysalis and birth results.

The Butterfly is trying to teach us that life is a never-ending cycle of self-transformation. The butterfly remind us that life is for improvement, as they feed on flowers they help pollinate, thereby changing and moving so gracefully being grateful for life good moments even if it's for a short time.

As for one of our flying friends the Crow is fascinated by its own shadow has amazing gifts they are called the left-handed guardian, the keeper of all sacred laws and it's been said they can bend the laws of the physical universe and shape shifting. Although this ability is rare and unique, the Crow signifies a firsthand knowledge of a higher order of right and wrong, than indicated by the laws created in human culture. Human law is not the same as Sacred Law. Crow is an omen of change, crow lives in the void and has no sense of time, crow sees simultaneously the fates, past, present and future. Crow merges light and darkness, seeing both inner and outer reality. As well as massager from the spirit world and is thought to dwell beyond the realm of time and space.

When you learn to allow your personal integrity to guide you, you will learn your reality and mission in life. Crow speaks of humanity need to honor the divine law, and stop being in denial of who you are and what you are destine to be in doing so, one honor ones future.

Now we come to one of the greatest player in society growth one of the fines qualities and nobility in a domesticated animal the" Horse."

Humanity made a leap forward when horse was domesticated, before Horses; humans were earthbound, heavy-laden, and slow moving creatures. Humanity owes the Horse a great debt of gratitude they carry burdens for mankind great distances and would not stop until it reached the destination or job was done. Even down though time the Horse has been misused, drug-up for racing to speeds that could break their hearts and if a leg would break in the run they would kill them for insurances. If you would learn or get information from the Humane Society you would see how often reports are send in of abuse to Horses. Once humans climbed on the Horse's back they took control, using them to no end abusing to no end.

The Horse is noted for it is strive for balance shield. And if you open your heart to find the teaching you will see the instrument of divine spirit of love in the horse and NO Abuse of power to the horse will bring wisdom.

In the Hindu tradition the chariot of Surya, the sun god, is pulled by stallions as is the chariot of Apollo Greek mythology. In Chinese astrology the horse is associated with appeal and persuasiveness. Horses are symbols of freedom. Do not forget the importance of the Horses people, are so easy to forget the important things in life.

In closing of this area, in an approach to the situation of the so-call filth of society that people want to ignore, but it's a reality which is facing all of us, its spanning.

In view of the main shame of society the criminals seem to be hopeless, in turning around their acts, although some are able to make changes for the better in reality even the criminals can be cultivated, only if they are willing to be.

In this world there are always, possibilities for change for the better. The need for encouragement in desire for growth, so many thinks about the situations at present but if encouraged the whole of society will benefit.

In vision of a better society no human-being is a lost cause. Knowing we are willing to give others a chance to change.

Exploring Beauty

We Humans must become conscious of the unlimited world around us, knowing we humans are just one part of the creation and it takes all part to make a whole.

Many of you are having a vacation from reality not taking into accord all life streams are channels to dwell within the Source of all life. These four-footed friends of humanity are apart of the earth challenge too. We humans must be mindful of what has been said about animals are lower creation or just 'dumb' old animals.

An animal deserves respect for what it is a true –friend to mankind in rendering tremendous services to us, they deserve our gratitude for the Source of life has permitted them to expand their love to us, and we should show appreciation for their love.

The Animal Kingdom is to be protected, not victimize for ones entertain. They are apart of the One Source as we humans are and there is no different in them and us as others in creation. Life is still life, think about this an animal can sense vibrations far ahead of the human and can alert to protect the human friend, why than respect this true friend.

Look close at the animal in your home the understanding that an animal lower than you should be out the question, these animals communicating with you although you are not understanding them, think about it, if you take an animal out of it natural habitat and made they part of your society the animal will object and capable of communicating with those who shelters it.

Be mindful of the love these animals show to us. Some of these animals sacrifice their lives to feed us and to protect us, so be mindful of your feeling about the animals.

So don't be so quick to entertain the thought as so many do that they have outlived their usefulness, and start miss-treating them or put them out to fend for themselves, never forget what goes round, will come around, understand animal are not the only ones came be placed in the streets.

Each species of animal, birds, reptiles etc., is under the supervision of a Diva in charge of their Group Souls, yes the animals have souls, and the Diva is responsible for directing each species for their survival, so you need to understand they are protected by a divine entity as we humans are protected.

A PRAYER FOR THE ANIMALS

HEAR OUR PRAYER O GOD FOR OUR ANIMALS FRIENDS AND BEING OUR REAL BROTHERS AND SISTER IN CREATION I ADDRESS THE LOVE FOR LIFE OF THESE DEAR SOULS TO FEEL FOR THEM AS DO ALL LIFE AS ONE.

A SPEACE PRAYER FOR THE ONES WHO ARE SUFFERING; FOR ALL THAT ARE OVERWORKED; UNDERFED; AND CRUELLY TREATED; AND THE ONES WHO ARE PUT TO DEATH BY HUMANS: WE SEND FORTH ALL THE MERCY AND PITY FROM THOSE WHO LOVE YOU AND CARE FOR YOUR BEING AND SOUL BE BLESS.

AND SO IT IS

INDIVIDUALITY

One may think it's the aggregate of qualities that distinguishes one person from another. Yes, this can be true in one sense there are other factors one must conceiver of each individual. First let's focus on what all people have in common, we all have consciousness, but we have individual memories of one's own self-experiences.

We only can arrive at the same eventuate by following others application of experiences as well as ones' own self-experiences in the moment to moment which supports our activity of the two.

Understand in the beginning ones conscious becomes aware of when we draw from the minds of others in the form of absorption of ideas, thoughts and imagination. We all take from others in developing our personality and virtues.

When a person develops and formula ideas and real knowledge he/she sought through others ideas and views taking with them the valued parts for a higher evolvement of one's true self and become an individual with the ability to think and reason for oneself, as one dedicate oneself every day to channel their minds for Divine guidance's. As one adopt the consciousness for the need for Divine guidance one will let the cosmic power express itself in ones personality as a self-confidence individual with their own minds and divine intervention.

Our conscious existence turns into a value of experiences and acting, which draws on the past which cause the surface mental memories to analysis for change. This grasping of memories from the past and acknowledging the fullness of the movement in which, the present pulls away from the past that appease to ones consciousness for keeping but opposes and have no use in that moment, one focus and determine to overcome the blankness of the future with all its uncertainties that tries to seize ones knowledge for stability in the movement in time toward an individuality that works for one's own quest in life.

The individuality of a person must take place in each of us in some period in time for the evolvement of our personal true- self. In order for one to receive higher knowledge from the great bank of Conscious existence and to utilize all values that is dominate one must seek the knowledge and remove ignorance that non-existence immobile status.

The individual is faced with a question to become directed in self-consciousness in the form of being a mental being who is aware of one's own existence as being one with the universe and one who can reason in truth or one who is being who is apart of the collective consciousness willing to follow every wind that blows of ideas and views that will not proper you for your evolvements?

We are to embrace truth that led to our individuality and self-consciousness pressing towards the future in the present for one's life divinity. Individuality may mean to somewhat separate one-self, from that dominating continent, overt constant builder of society with its imperfections.

First one must receive wholeness with you requires, which will open the door for self-realization, this will bring you to the path you must follow to your true-self, which will cause you to become conscious of your true essence and individualizes

To be an individual one must become an advance unaffected by the distinction of the past, present or space and circumstance. Think about it, as we become aware of the stable self in becoming a self-realize person, one who think for themselves, not moved by every wind that flow one's mind with suggestions and every river that floods ones emotion, but one who is capable of taking the right course of action to better ones life and able to be detach from the illusion of others, being one who are determine for greatness in their own individualizes expression in ones our.nature

We, as human beings are relative, eternal substance of existence, we look forward to seeing behind the mental flow of a differentiated of self-experience, knowing the eternal soul-substance behind the mental formation of one as self-ego is a evolving consciousness and behind the mentality it moves into the eternal present where it work for that individual.

The surface consciousness of an individual is constantly adding and rejecting from suggestions and experiences, also modifying both. Although the deeper characteristic of the individual remains to support the outer superficial self.

In reality people are constantly developing though their experiences, so basely the individual conscious come into power to empower self-control, even when the changes within the body, the surrounding empowerment is not so insistent obvious, the mentality only regard it as a produce effect upon its own mental consciousness.

In order to generate impressions and change the mental experience and mental body one's mind must be open to become aware of its changes in physical and mental habits in their surrounding experiences.

With the extension of our minds or I should say, consciousness, we can obtain the ultimate discovery of what our own highest deepest vastest self in our individuality.

These acts of discovery will be the root to an enjoyable life that liberates one from blocks of marble hard creations brought through many years or lifetimes of commitment to unproductive and unrewarding activity.

Happiness exists within one's own self first as a private disposition, and then expands out into the world to be shared by other persons.

Individuality brings ones self-image to value, with the intent to produce the maximum results for prosperity in all areas of life. The ultimate goal is not to sacrifice one's true self, knowing nearly everyone's social, political, or theological views are influence by ones environment, this trance one must not be consumed, which may cause a projection of ugliness.

The ultimate desire is to destroy the mental slavery which stops the dreamers from dreaming of a better life on earth and not trying to escape from our heritage of who and what we are in this world.

Yes it's important to evolve to be the best we can be as human beings, there is a "but" we must clean-up our past first and then move on to higher levels in the evolutional stage. And the first step is to become an individual in the sense of morality and values, understanding we all are one in the sense as being human, we all must make the same choices to exert the effort to be honest to integrate with reality, and to think and be rational in our daily lives to serve.

The individual is one who thinks for oneself and rationalizes always with the ability to survive and self-supportive value system in place. Their inescapable identification of what must be done and what one must not do, as their wide integrated thought-system makes the way for complete survival.

Individuals will not permit others to manipulate or attack the credibility of honesty and truth. There are those who attack values to gain control and power over the weak- minded ones. The true individual stands their ground.

Being an individual is not enough in the sense of the word, even the best intentions are important without sound ideas and effort is needed to elevate the ideas to be worthy of higher value level which brings improvement. Ideas alone cannot provide competence and self-esteem to the point of leadership roll it takes effort to move up to higher levels to assist others to gain their place in their evolvement and understand, each of us have a responsibility to help our fellow-man to evolve to their next level.

All accomplishment comes with the understanding of what one must abandon the old dark non-productive ideas of dishonesty which causes deterioration of one's personal true fabrics.

The concept for accomplishment on an individual bases is through the motivation of oneself on a personal level in the form of control of self to gain profitable advantages from any situation. Becoming a powerful person in identifying who and what you are.

Question, how does one translate their real self? Do you see yourself as a healthy, strong, youthful person or do you feel weak, depressed or an unwanted by others? I guess that's two questions; in true reality the question are a part of each other.

It's amazing to reveal people to their own minds, to raise invisibility to the visible level to receive a new view of one-self or should I say true self image visible to consciousness. From the moment you become conceive with what you really think about yourself you come to the precision of shaping your invisible blueprint of your future destiny to improve the flow of your life unlimited vigor and energy.

.   Many first impression of the question asked are operated on the limited level of one's body and mind of what one look for in the physical or one's intellect, picturing others look better or educated more then you. You select the physical and outer visible accepted view of what you should be. Which other have directed as acceptable to their liking?

Let's be real only you can judge yourself, it's all about you, keys to explore the vision of worthiness of oneself is first to love yourself. And to access the power within you to see your worthy one must bring the lower-self in balance with the higher-self, it's a spiritual-process to become your higher-self, which is your real self or one can say your original self or perfect as in the beginning.

For those who are not familiar with the terms lower-self and higher-self, let us defined exactly what is meant by the terms. First the lower-self is that part of a person natural senses to feel emotions, create patterns to live by in the materialist areas and give into thoughts, dissatisfaction, resentment, jealousy, greed, hatred, etc., also the functions from the lower three Chakras. The higher-self, is the part of the individual which believes to be the so-call image of God or the Universal Mind via the silver cord to the head and run along the spinal column in the Kundalini the subconscious mind, and brings pure information from the Christ Consciousness it exist as pure Spirit, your spirit.

Which functions are of both cause and effect, in harmony with the atoms intelligence or one can say Bionomic energy or one's life experience perceived through intuition an inward intuitive direction guiding and individual through life on a higher level. As for the word Kundalini it expresses itself when a person is unconscious of it it's a power or force following winding or circular pathway carrying or conveying thought originating in the higher triad.

Enough, about this area, we must receive insight to who we are and practice that truth we can be free as an individual. One must improved oneself if we see the need. Character building respect oneself first and constantly improve in ones virtues.

NATURE'S LOVE

It's been taught down through the ages repeatedly about love, in what one should feel, think and act, in receiving and giving of love.

This may sound strange to you, but I welcome the true meaning of love. Now please listen attentively.

This area is importance it's the first thought that one should torch ones mind in understanding Love. The Source of love is oneself and the true Source of life. People seek love basely from others outside of their selves, not feeling really knowing what's true love is. People have not understanding ones Source and oneself are first in the line for real love. By not knowing if you do not love your- self first one can not trustfully love others. Those persons who are not lovers of oneself are unloved in a sense by not knowing how to love so they feel unloved by others. There are many reasons for this type of mind-frame.

Let's speak on some of the reasons; in making the past, and presence situations and experiences, cause a breakdown and control of future development of ones conception of the true love for oneself. The sub-conscious has stored according to what's programmed. As one receive instruction and one develops one Instinet from past events in ones life, ones blind intelligence to ones personal world.

We understand by what been told to us about love; the love of a mate, love of family and love of friends and the love for humanity, etc., All has no true meaning if one has no love for oneself first and ones Creator. First the creator is all ways first that goes without question or saying.

We cannot accomplish the wonderful conception of true without these feelings for the self and the Source of life first. One must forgive the past clear out the subconscious mind. One must condition yourself on a purpose for your life, just for you in self love. How can you love others without loving oneself first?

First I thank you for the privilege of being one of these persons who will assist those who desire to be helped in opening one's mind to the realization or the real truth of what love is in a more broader sense.

There guise differences between true love and false love. Let's speak on a love we all can understand, real love is deep within us in our Christ-Self, it comes from what we human's call "heaven's Realms," which brings true freedom, it reaches up into the glorious storehouse of all giving of good.

Mankind in their ignorance is farther away than he ever dreamed because of their self-identification with the superficial, their body and they seem to be determined by their emotional body to or are preoccupy with physical gratification as being love.

In knowing, that we are loved beyond the touching and feeling of the matter that we embody, It's a state of being, an indeterminate, perhaps indeterminable existence, beyond the manifestation of being and both through that movement of one's nature.

We pursue the process of what many say love is but we should seek truth of what is true love. Every individual seek love in difference ways, family first, romantic and love of god or creator and still seek a relationship with self.

Now as for the false love, that sexual feeling which begin before puberty, very young children and babies two and three months old have sexual experiences as noted by Freud and Kinsey in a study. Young children experience sexual stimulation by bath being handling, caring, or fondling, sometimes it may becomes a form of abuse, a situation where such pleasures can often inhibited by incest fears and taboos, parents, or kin or caregiver, will misuse their privileges to the child. Valid sensuous sexual pleasures can be experienced between child and mother during nursing or nude cuddling, some time cuddling can be a loving, healthy and benefiter to the child, it can make the child feel a generous act of love, but one must take care of its limit experience, because children are not develop sufficiently to know what is forbiddance and what approached, it's up to the adult or matured person who has been permitted to care for the child to stop before things get out of hand.

Let's talk about adults uses of that sexual concept because the average person thinks a romantic love is based on sex, question if sexual activity is no longer possible, now where is the love gone?

I need to start somewhere, so I will start with the adolescent as I said the adolescents or children are not sufficiently developed, or understand the deep emotional involvements and the serious mutual commitment with sexual partners.

Not only are the adolescents, but many adults are having the same problems, regardless of age. The casual sexual relationships undermine ones values and self-esteem by given away ones personal power in giving into ones harmful pleasures. I should explain, if one gives away their will like having sex because someone else desires it not you own desire you give in because you don't want that other person to be disappointed or you are willing to receive favor in someone's eyes or to gain financially you are violating yourself.

People are seductive behind every relationship sexual or otherwise there is or real reason for the relationship it is either a healthy or an unhealthy motive. Since no one can know everything, so they make mistakes in the beginning of the relationship as they grow in their involvement with their partner the potential for improves manifest hopefully, what determines a successful relationship is the combine effort of creativity and the respect for each other and their space.

Let' get back to the real subject of the love of nature, we humans are so far behind in the real purpose and reason for love, it's not about sex or controlling each other by desire or force, love is something each of us need to understand by submitting to it.

All feeling and emotions fluctuate, in every type of relationship even the non-romantic, that what people focus their attraction now.

Some may think I have the words out of order, but think about this, love of nature, it's meaning love is manifested in nature, as we submit to the nature of love, we ask ourselves what really is the nature of love.

We know that every various gradation and types of being come into existence by love for the nature of that incarnated gradation or type of being and the nature itself is love in itself. And love is a fundamental manifestation placed in matter which creates a nature of that substance, by the consciousness of something higher than us and beyond our comprehensions gauge. The real idea is to build it through one's own conscious-force to be able to create one's own nature to love.

Though the indwelling spirit for the lack of a better word, the spirit of love directs and creates nature, although a basic similarity of line may be visible, the creative power might use not one but many processes or set many forces to act together. We see with our eyes the love of nature as it's called, the progress of love though natures from matter to life, from life to mind in reality of its love working though nature. We do not think of love as imaginable, we know it is real. Someone said there is no proof that matter developed into life or life-energy in matter is mind-energy, understand mind is living matter and it is a manifestation of love.

Love is determinate to influence the many activities of nature; we fine in our subjective experiences on the physical plane the impressions of events, habits, fixed mental psychological content impressions which form our opinion about life.

The body's function is a necessary machinery or instrumentation for the movement of mental inhabitant; it is only by setting the instrument in motion that the conscious being emerges though the evolving of its nature of love, it can formats and turn a mask of matter into a manifestation of conscious being.

We look at nature with a certain difficulty as for understanding its mechanical works, or the relative discover of formulas of the pure reason, not looking at the mystic vision or the spiritual without that inner vision of realities only will the abstraction of the formulation of natures love in shown.

The universes are a manifestation of an infinite and eternal All-Existence; The Divine Being dwells in all that is, and that being is known as Love and it shows its love in nature's workings. Whiter divine, human, animal, plant, minerals, and forces and motion all have their own forms of activity in their nature.

Let's look more carefully into the form of nature, most people think of nature being the patterns of geometrical forms which has projected upon it and the working of logical laws.

The mechanical order of things it in the form of cause and effect and being with our limitations for thought only to the secondary or the relative comprehensive mentality.

We are limited, because we have chose to be, if one closes their mind to the presence thought as being alienated by the universe, the universe will open up and a deeper description of nature will be vision.

By us humans haven the notion we can control the image of things and it blindsides others of receiving the images of natures goods, many think nature is superficial in its make-up itself. It seem strange when other parts of or nature receive the attention in the form of love and goodness from the source of the love for its nature acted upon in a spontaneity given of that love and the nature of the things reacts inwardly with joy and by showing outwardly in beauty of it form.

The love of nature is extended inwardly and the entity or matter of form becomes an object of that love with knowledge and fully aware of the inseparable love which controls life of all things in itself. This love is so perfect that it's beyond control.

Love is something one cannot control or take hold for only oneself
It's something one cannot lose, or steal from another
It cannot be hidden by darkness it brings light in all dark places
You cannot silent the cry for it, we will die without it
This Love for all natures is beyond all thought and comprehension.

REALITY OF LIFE

In the preceding chapters it has been written for the average person communicative level, this chapter is the one I will not expect every reader to accept or have complete and immediate understanding of all of the concepts that are presented in this work. Therefore included are some elements hopefully will enlighten all levels of the awareness to the ordinary reader?

One of the most important things in life is for one to be open to learning. Ignorance is the most insidious type of bondage which those who are imprison in unawareness of their chains, and not being willing to learn or open-up to what is before them, things which governs one's life, that is causing one to be a prisoner of ignorance and a slave to the ignorant views of others without a clue of the forces that are not working in one's favor or supports ones life for the better. Another thing it raises from the most insistent demands of mankind, the desire for security, well-being, peace, and harmony. Humans are pressed by many ills, famine, and other natural disasters the evils, because of the ignorance in mankind, and the inhumane acts towards other fellow-humans and other forms of life.

Humans should be more than mere creatures of their environment and outside influences because one is a Sub- Divine creature in the making. One should be ruled by the inner Divine-Power, instead of merely a weak instrument of others desires, and influences which can cause one to become just a slave to all suggestions and impressions, from every passing person or thing other than your own desires and emotional feelings of your real-self.

We humans should direct our minds to open to the power within us, to be truthful to oneself in determination to be, what our true purpose in life as a (mirror of Divinity). To open to the endeavor with attainment of that inner Power from within we must become one with the causes of that power.

Humanity is living in difficult times, the flourishing of evil behind the acts of false intention of some of mankind in their disconnection from the true realities in life.

Remember truth will set you free, and the purpose should be to increase harmony love and happiness in each and every form of life on the planet. If every human being would be willing to open to the Love and respect of life, the realities of life will come clear.

Existing without true understanding is a crime toward your self. How can you have wholeness in oneself if you are filled with unknowingness and insecurity about real life, it's like being a ripper of non-time and one is focused without a true destination, not seeing the need to free one-self from outer conditions that does not serve humanity and other entities in life. Exaltation into its greatest purpose, then you have not tasted or touched the magic within yourself.

An attempt has been made in the preceding chapters to draw your attention to the problems of the past to reform ones individual consciousness. Because of some individuals who chose not to evolve in consciousness or become isolated, in their generated interest in non-productive activities, the chance to evolve is hard for those individuals. They suffer in time do to their activities which brings unworthy results in unwilling to follow the moralities set in place by Spiritual and Philosophical blueprints of wisdom traditions.

Humankind has become captivated in what many believe to be a good life. Understand one must release the thought that all people have a functioning morals life. All do not use morality in their lives from day to day. Many believe or see morals in different ways from you and I believe it to be different cultures think differently about morality, for some it's only an illusion and not a reality of life.

Whatever mankind thinks and feels, creates in manifestation of that thought or emotional act generates through the power of those thoughts to create at will, that's their reality, if it is good it's okay, if not many feel that's still okay. Therefore all the mistakes of the past existent to this age revealing in the form of bygone ignores as a drop in the ocean of endless time, infilling the inhabitants on this earth.

Now for those who desire to go beyond what has been taught in the sense of theology as we think about things it, what do we really know, what is reality to you? We are not man originated from animals, animals originate from us, it may seem odd to say because It's been said the opposite though the opinion of Darwin, but do we know the reality of life in its true- form. When the universe reaches a point, there's a law that expands into a phenomenon world that maintenance the true realities in life.

Now let's go a little deeper for those who really want to go deeper into the realities in the so-call life experience as being, beyond the first materiality cause experience.

In the great Life-Cycle on earth of the fourth round only the mammalian, were the animals with a vertebrate skeleton and reproductive functions which from the beginning up to present have continued to be more or less like our own, and they underwent same cyclical changes in their structure and functional systems that we as humans in our evolutionary enfoldment.

We look at life as a journey, in time (Reality) depends on our environment, our compare the real to the un-real it always dependent on ones own point of view. The time comes when you need to challenge ones own reality. In so doing one must not take everything at face value, ask your selves, if you like the reality you are living now?

Lets speak of some thing we see is reality; everything must play their role in life birth, death, and rebirth, look at it like this; "We are in the eternal return and each one is to play their given role.

Let us explore the thought of what many people avoid asking of themselves "who am I," why am I here." Question; what is it, in the non-verbal sense just in the silent observation, can it be in the moment or in clarity of the mind, whereby one becomes open to their own individual reality? Can it be in the time when on listening to that inner-voice the true nature of one's person, that we become separated into individualize consciousness of the self purpose in the sense of character to work our own plan or purpose. But we are one in reality, just as we are in a part of the "Oneness of the All". What I am saying, or getting too is one must understand this comes back to the "Oneness of Existence" that one is to awaken too. We are surrounded by the miracle and magic of life, which brings all reality into play, why not tap into it, and the influence of true reality take its place in your life?

Stop being motivated by non-constructive activity, feel the regulating of your heart, and the bloodstream and metabolism perfectly in you it's time to be concern about other life forms as well all are one in creation.

First in order to respect something one must know what it is in its realness, now let's think of life as it is to you, many only think it's just a physical vehicle to act out your desires and dreams good or bad! Others think it's an invisible energy moving around in space of the earth etc., what do you think?

Let's envision some of the concepts that constitute the thoughts about life. Another question, are we humans living in an illusion world in the concepts about life or are there a real meaning to this what we call life?

Respect for life is inspirited through the spark of life. The great Source of life which creates all things, knows everything, including how you are going to react at every moment, what is required of you is for you to govern your life in such a way that you will know your every move to the point that you are in control of your own destiny.

By being in control you will lose interest in the things that are not good for you and others as- well. The magic in life is gradually losing interest in the things that hold you back from a successful life. Now having a successful life means different things to different people, what I call a successful life is being healthy in body, mind and spirit. When you have those things you can achieve all other things you desire overtime.

Please understand if you use the divine energy negatively or for an evil purpose there will not be total success in your life it may appear to be good but in the long run is will fail. Do not let the people applause you for wrong doing. You see they are not the ones who will pay the price for the wrong activities you will, and don't think because you are doing it for your boss in a company or you country it's all the same, it's the law of attraction, as they say "what goes around, comes around,"

Always demonstrate the best character as possible, it will become a habit and enter the subconscious mind where it will receive for memory.

There are people who feed on unworthiness to deceptive others, because they think that is the real world, or it's been what they have been taught from childhood and thinks it's the only way to receive, but they do not know they have developed their own destiny.

There are people who has been brought up in negative environments as a child, who adepts to that environment with no interest in change, but there are many who has the same background by removing them self from the unwanted elements and become very successful in development of their own person and a asset to society that child will be different then his//her environment, because the person becomes whole and know what their life mean to them. There are some may take more time to grow than others and some live their whole life with no change. These are the comfortable ones in their now state and so that opinions can be right for some persons not all only the ones with no desire rarely do they move from that which they know, but there are those who explore other plane, to receive a better life, ones of nobility. One can only hope they become worthy persons, and not worse to prove a point, or they reflect unworthy patterns in their adulthood from their families environment as a child began with drinking to the point of becoming a chronic alcoholic and problems with other forms of substances, all of this lead to an unbalance person.

In order for humankind to become one with life as we relatively understand life

To be, one must unify one's characterized by quality of good effect. The consequence of all activity interplay with the substance of life based on the central life evokes and the manifested consciousness, or awareness of response to all that is eventuating, but in degree which is somewhat impossible for all to comprehend by many of the humankind development or evolvement in. their consciousness.

As for the present development of mankind it's somewhat limited in the relative concern, we humans make judgment –call about others and other form of life and their ability to understand to think or to make discussion, we as humans should stop feeding into the appearances of falseness of what we think we know and open up to the reality of life and all its wonders we would be better off. And most of all condition us to the factors of life's qualities.

Always there are predicate that which stands outside of appearances and in order to be conscious or to evolves awareness of its material development and consequent adequacy of expression and awareness of its enfoldment to grasp one must train ourselves to regard ourselves as an undeveloped expression and reflection of the initial creative quaternary of life.

We as humans live making an appearances expressing quality and slowly becoming more like that of our destine plan in place for us which is becoming more of the reflection of Divinity in perfection itself.

Let's speak about the respect for what we seen to think is lesser in creation or intellects. The animal kingdom, vegetation kingdom, and the geological rocks and soils and the elements like the Sun and Moon and stars in the sky, The Air and Water, also the Gemstones within the earth, many look on these species of life as unimportant, but they are very wrong.

All living creatures play a large portion in this plan of life. We all must open our minds and let knowledge come in about the reality of life.

Not to move far off the main subject I will shorten my examination; we humans of today are not in the third-round or the First and/or Second-Root Race like those who were not as we understand to be ones with the degree of self-consciousness intelligence and ability to reason and use moral judgment, it has been said, they were mindless, much like little children just as today little children are mindless to a degree, not meaning, however that our children lack mental capacity in latency, or rather the potentially of their minds. Their mind begins to manifest itself and progressively over the years while the child is growing and their functions and qualities, operations of mentality they inherent the power of mind.

It may be just as-well for the sake of clarity to round out briefly the aspects of mind or consciousness.

That which, existence in human beings we can find two major modes of consciousness; one is analytic, and the other holistic. The first analogous to process of viewing in the individual is parts and second to viewing at once the whole. Humans receive knowledge through the rational and the intuitive sides of their nature. In mankind intellectual growth and history, many have separated these two modes of knowing into science and religion, for example the two differ in their concerns and their rarely commerce with the other. Science has become the dominated influence in our culture.

Understandably the religion orders are showing mirrors of immorality, and devaluing the need for the evolvement of the human-soul. With the breakdown of the religion as a major cultural force by many of different orders, it's natural to turn to other approaches, and then the ideal of scientific knowledge has become the dominant mode of knowledge within our culture.

Even in the two major modes of consciousness, we are taught precious little about our emotions, our bodies or our intuitive capabilities. There are a emphasis on verbal, intellectual knowledge has filtered out much of what could be appropriate for study in contemporary psychology and others systems which use other methods to connect to higher sources of knowledge like using meditation which are much misunderstood; the experience of the "non-ordinary realities" is not studied because they do not fit into the dominated paradigm. Current psychology is undergoing first stirring of a synthesis of the two modes. These may form the beginning of a more complete science of human consciousness with an extended conception of our own capabilities.

This new conception of the human possibilities is no way a new one it's been use for many years by the eastern civilization, it's the ancient wisdom tradition, and the different is many believe it's a new technology of contemporary science.

There is a poem by the Persian Sufi mystics, translated by English scholar Nicholson as follow: "Lo *for I to myself am unknown; now in God's name what must I do? I adore neither the cross nor the crescent; I am not Glamour of a Jew. East nor West, land nor sea is my home, I have no kin nor with angel gnome, I am wrought not of fine nor of form, I am shaped neither of dust nor dew. I was born not of china afar, not in Sassing and not in burgher; not in India, where five rives are, nether neither Iraq nor Kherson I grew. Not in the world I dwell, not in paradise nether in hell; not from Eden and rid wan I fell not from Adam my lineage I drew In a place beyond utter most places in attract without shadow or trace, soul and body transcending I live in the soul of my loved One anew."*

To understand what has been said here in this poem, one must read beneath the lines and seize the inner thought. The only clue I can give is the Divine Source of which he sings, the Divine, is the Source of us all, when we shall finish our evolutionary journey successfully and rise to our own perfection state of our existence, we become, one with all creations in the same dwelling place of the Most High, the Source of it all.

In order to understand the activities in the world socialites today we must present more information regarding the influences of the non-productive suggestive societies of the lower inferior minds of people who haven't leveled to the point of enrollment of the human stage on the ladder to the relative perfection of the human-being.

In order to truly understand these activities that is being systematic in due to the intelligent individuals of many great communities worldwide

Let's move along back to respect of all life, many people have problems in respect for oneself not even speak of others, it comes down to one being conscious of self, I know I speak of the consciousness all through this book, it's because of the importance the need to understand we all have apart in this universal game of learning. We vision the phenomenological part of being, we look among the different forms of life as being subjective and objective as far as consciousness is concern. Let's open our minds think of the things that separates us from each other is the way we communicate.

Among all living beings there are problems in communication at times even people of different counties. So how much would it is for different species to communicate?

There is a barrier between species in the form of language, as the results of the barrier; the form beings in their different form are labeled as inferred ones deprived of consciousness and unable to communicate; example, plants, since believed they do not have a system of vital relations and they only commutate by attributes to certain sensibility which is collective their specific thrust of their growth, perseverance, or reproduction.

There are reviews in non-technical prose with examples, of the complex behavioral patterns in animal, plants, as we know or believers' earth so-call life was first developed in salt water of the seas to control any living cell from the high salt ions level of sodium chloride, by restriction it s movements in and out of living cell. The cell is covered with thin skin, the cell membrane, which is a fatty layer insulating the inside of the cell from environment. Not going into details it's too much and takes me away from the subject into other areas. To say this, not only I believe other life forms van feel and can communicate we are unable to communicate with them.

As for the animals, it's believed that sensibility is their movements of expression and commutate, and their behaviors be understood to as form of mechanical and they respond to stimuli by reactions, in which they are capable not only of moving themselves under the influence of tropism or instincts but also of being able to postpone the objective of their desires, overcome obstacles and dispel dangers..

Even the so-called lower-animals species have self-determination of choice, of adaptation or motivation by employed objective ethnology appears.

The average human logically speak of the consciousness level of other species of life, as inferior to us humans, but the most hideous thing is that people believe that computers know other then what had been program in it, not getting off the subject, but I asked a man on the phone why I was being called by his company, the man said, I do not know, but the call was made by their computer, so the man said to me, "the computer called you "the computer knows," if the average person thinks like the man that I talk to computer knows more than a person who made it, something is real wrong with society and we are in deep trouble, if one think a machine knows more than relative life forms.

Know This, Animals and other life forms are not inferior, to us but the machines are inferior because man made them, only thing we humans or animals are inferior is the commutative barrier is in place and because of that's a known fact. This is why we as humans should study them more, not by torture or killing or discarding the fact that they are created for a purpose as you and I, by the Source of life, not by humans.

Understand all have their self-consciousness or self-governing factors.

So we come to the reality that all is "consciousness" the so-call lower species plants, animals, insects, vegetation, minerals, and all that share this earth are a form of consciousness whereas the lower species necessitates the presence of at least sensibility, memory and an organization, which enhances their certainty of being.

The average human make light of the other forms of life, their zoo-consciousness or neurobiological consciousness, they too have subjective and objective determination.

We human fail to understand although we all are using a system called the vital relations in organized and the central nervous system, we attribute consciousness. They show themselves no different from us in the ability to organize whatever is needed to make their individual situation work for them.

Tell me "why "has humankind separated themselves from other forms of life, simply because of language barriers?

We human fear what we cannot understand, placing a label on it, as inferior, deprived, or evil.

Let's move into another area the Ancient philosophers looked at the world's inhabitants and saw its diversity and the seemly chaos of things and looked to see the primary first principle which means the unity and order to be given to all in their differences.

Even in this day and time so-call civilizations or what we call humanity are still static beings. Humanity is working against the universal plan.

We who desire change for better are looking for change in the transformation shape and form of the human consciousness, knowing everything in reality "changes."

We must always seek change to be in a constant state of becoming rather than a state of static being. The entire universe is never the same from moment to moment so why should we be different in our form we too are subject to the changing process from one instant to the next.

It doesn't matter how hard one fight to arrest the changes there will be changes taking place in all areas in this relative stage of life. Why are people so afraid of change?

Why should anyone be afraid of change! What can be more rewarding and suitable for all life than change? It's the universal nature of life to change. Understand there is nothing more useful than change, for without change life would have no meaning.

All particles of matter soon disintegrate into the substance of the Whole; and every form of life with cause integrates into the memory of the Source of the All, things, causing face of eternity.

In reality our universal nature is to be one with all relative life. The persons feel cut off from other forms of life or far removed from us, is because our lives are more artificial, synthetic way. The natural rhythm of life is far removed from us by our own making.

One must come to the reality in regard to all universal life is a single living being, having one main Source or substance which relates to all forms of creation in the cosmic-consciousness of this one Source, that all life shares in.

Observe how everything moves with is impulse, to create whatever is required of it at time of movement. All of nature is the same whether their make-up of stone, plants, animals or human bodies, all are one in life.

As I was writing this book, I became more awaken and in touch with life as a whole. As I breathe a feeling of inseparability came when I thought on other species. My insight had developed to perceptively all life as intertwine of textures and patterns with many colors all different but of the same garment, and I desired to receive more insight to the mystery of life.

The majority of people of earth explore life in the uncharted land of pain and pleasure, but their thinking has remained clouded by assumptions formed in a primitive world. The life forms are speaking; can you hear, obviously it is hard to believe, but life has always been speaking to us only few are listening to its voices. One does not need to feel pain of ignorance only make mind extension in ones attitude about other life forms.

Some may say there is language banner, of communication between species, yes but understand they understand us whatever language we speak. Question, have you wondered" Why"? Language only limits perception when its terms are taken too seriously. When one open to life in all its beauties and stop taking lightly its wonders in the different forms of nature. Society has been conditioned to see only life forms of earth though a filter of the past, murky glass of mammalian wants and desires only to repeat errors of history, forgetting that life changes and we as being a part of life must change too. The old habits of past must be given open to change as-well for the new perception of life.

To fully awaken to the earth inhabitants it requires willingness to be open to life and all it brings in the form of love for it. See the love in a blade of grass, dull, a passing cloud, in a Squirrel, a house, and a bird singing a song an oak tree and feel the wind and rain on your face.

Humankind thoughts are giving over to being superior to other life forms, but in reality not true, because we think by being told that we are does not make it so, if you study other species some are more loving and compassion's than humans so one cannot assume humans are superior to other life forms. It is. A banner between us yes, hopefully it's the spiritual make-up, but that too may be misapplied.

We can no longer overlook the potential or underestimate their uniqueness. I want you to think about this, when you was in grade-school there were some who pass to the next grade and there was some did not, understand if humans do not pass what is required than other forms will take it up and pass over the human form. It up to the individual who will pass and to still go in circles lifetime after life time not moving upward or forward in their evolvement toward the required plan.

Humans have influence the earth more than any other species. More often than not our historical events have influence has been destructive. Our survival has been destructive. Our survival and the survival of countless species now hinges on making changes in consciousness that will end this cycles for the better hopefully.

In ones natural state of being though is not sense of identity distinct from ones creator except when one is engaged in a relationship. On this level of being identity comes into focus only in the context of a relationship, with some other aspect of being that has become an objective.

The reality is when you are called forth from the atom into material matter in the form of human flesh with a heart, and brain, the divine impulse calls upon your service and brings you into form to encounter other being (species) of life and variety on errands and excursion a world of love with holes of light that are impossible to describe.

In so doing you realize the certainty of your oneness with the Source (Absolute manifestation) of your creation.

As you become aware of the truth about whom you really are, and not until than will you really know that all are one in the relative life is so doing stop living a dual expression of what life it.

After the fall humankind also other species developed what is call diuretic reality, where you encounter both identity experiences for the duration of one life on this planet. With this dual identity one still is aware one's unity with the Creator (Source).

At first before the fall, one had the ability to shift the center of your awareness from diet to identity, from form to meta-form at will. One was free to emphasize whatever situation is required at the time. Understand all creatures share the same reality.

Maybe, I should example the fall it's the fall from grace, as mankind stated to believe that he knows best what is to be for their lives and the results a being without a clue.

Let's talk about the invisible tremendous power that creates beyond our understanding, that power or energy that makes beautiful forms of life, it works in the earth in a timely fashion, this power or energy develop life in nature. You see it working in the soil releasing at springtime from a seed becoming a fruit or vegetable and or a full grown gain in the summer, all of this tremendous work is done though powers beyond our understanding, in all mankind doing they still cannot bring thing in existence. We can ask that things can be done from the actual Creator, we only can make conditions right for the development of the crops of life, but not create, knowing it take the powers of creation to perform the work, knowing still without the sunshine, air, and water to bring to perfection whatever was in the seed it still beyond our control of the tremendous energy power of life.

We humans take life for granted, in small ways or large ways, not saying all, the scale is unbalance. Let's think about what would be like if just one of the elements was no longer operational for our survival, you can imagine the chaos.

Let's get personal, if one of your senses stop working let say the sense of smell which register contact with minute particles of objects into one nostril from the air which send messages to your Brain you're unable to breath in that substance, because the Air stop giving of itself, what would you feel? If this element was no longer resign in the earth call what would happen to us? The chemical composition will on longer be contacted. Do you realize there is nothing created in life without a purpose, all the more reason to respect all for it purpose.

This is why one admit change is in order, in doing so one becomes open to the world around us like a seed buried in the ground that once was dormant, now able to fashion one-self in the beauty of that seed which comes into full manifestation by the light of ones Sources of life. We humans must stop being in a dreamlike state and respond to the needs of all life.

Humankind can only manipulate the seeds of life, only have power to or maintain and manage the growth but not create. Does anyone think that the all Knowing Power would entrust the cosmic power in the hands of a group of egocentric and un-evolved creatures like humanity in the stage they are now?

First, let me example, this reflection is not on the ones who are beautiful people, or those who are highly good in character and would not harm anyone or anything but only do good at every opportunity, these are the ones who are marked with the manifested enfoldment to expand to make their own individual ascension form in a short time.

Many of the human family has programmed their subconscious with non-productive activities, and the awareness is not there of their condition. Mentally ones have to set their mind to seeking the cosmic light and ask for truth to guard their individual world.

Each morning when you arise, look at your body and say to yourself "this is good and I am so great-full to be here. I program into my higher mind qualities of only good, high morality, love and unselfishness." People forget that one must acknowledge the giver of your being in the form of appreciation for yet being thought of.

Humanity future destiny is in the results of their own individual evolvement.

If humanity would stop being preoccupied with non-productive activity and be willing to unlock the power of imagination and visualization for only good to come to them, knowing everyday passes with greater accomplishments.

As it stand in today world many are subjective to many unworthy emotions like greed, self-pity, hatred, anger, remorse and others not named, but I think you get the picture. The damage which these types of emotions have caused humanity to become blind to the reality of what life is.

All life-forms on this planet have been a seed of some-type and placed on the surface of this planet from somewhere else in this large out pull of the galaxy so all have a special purpose.

Some humans feel they are justify in bearing resentment against someone they believe harmed them or they ought to hate someone who hates them. There are events that are questionable which have occurred in the last fifteen years that if the people were given the truth about them it would have changed the course of history. What most people think or feel creates an atmosphere that passes from one to the other, and when they look back at it they do not remember where is started from they just keep passing one to another without a justification. It's the same with hate without a cause for someone or something without understanding.

Many humans do not know how to communicate on the positive wavelengths because they have been working the negative for so long their mind have attained to it.

But there are steps to change, by becoming magnetically attuned with great minds of other ages that are the master teachers and have evolved like Jesus of the Christ-Consciousness, Buddha etc., in so doing one's mind connects to the Cosmic mind power which will reveal the true reality about Love, and you will discover the hidden treasure and power to achieve a great destiny in the positive refinement of your new way of thinking.

Human's lives are in a veritable of space of cosmic mind power which surrounds us and brings the mystical forces to our relative understanding which many seldom use. These higher mind energies are cosmic subconscious motivators, by stopping being controlled by the non-productive mind-set which has based itself in ones subconscious-mind, the only change one has is to reprogram oneself into ones higher mind centers and know that this cosmic power which can be used to accomplish great things in your life.

The first thing one must do is know that "desire," is the key factor and automatic responses of one's higher level of subconscious mind, as a result will cause the release of positive power and create good for your life, knowing it's all about life.

It's been said that we humans are the guardians of other life-forms on earth, but is that so? Think about it, all animals, insects and birds operate under the automatic instinctive mind which causes them to do what is right to preserve them and perpetuate of their species. They are motivated from within their random instinctive intuition sense so what is the different in the animal and mankind it's all life motivated. We humans are motivated to override the laws in place set by the Source of life. Many cannot secure their own emotions or their mental state, would you want these people in control of your destiny?

I want to change the subject a little! Let's go to the beginning of the so-call creation of human- life on this planet (earth), our attention is focus on the event referred to as the "Temptation," first one must understand, with all the scattered records of that era yet remain, and we know that during the actual period of the Temptation only extant records were given by revelation at a time much later than the actual events occur themselves.

In the Judeo-Christian Bible, reference to a when the "Sons of God looked upon the Daughters of man," understand, many have been at a loss to the true interpretation of this passage, the best recounts in question was in the book of Enoch, but the work was rejected by the early churchmen hen deciding what the Bible would contain.

Man was created in human form 10 million years before the present state of mankind, the so-call first humans were immune to the law which now in place, we now are subject to ageing and death, wherein their initial state they did not age or die.

They did not have souls at that time in the sense of a continuing spark capable of surviving the disintegration of the physical body. These men at that early period were not differentiated sexually. Each entity included both male and female characteristics in roughly equal proportion. The laws of creation were obeyed because of that time was of innocents. In representation symbolically in Genesis by the garden of Eden, where Adam, before Eve was formed from one of Adam ribs, which symbol of the hermaphrodite human, with both sexes in the same body. Let's get to the part of the Temptation, where after sufficient period of acclimatization to the earth condition. Was decided by the entities who's had been given charge of the human group to initiate the next phase, which was the "Temptation."

The temptation era came in when it was decided that the time of innocence had run its course. The next step was the plan to prepare the humans and the other forms of life to change, no-longer will there be hermaphroditic individual but all would be divided into male and female in all species and though the separation they receive individual consciousness which by decision making it bring pain and suffering. By the so-call entity Lucifer volunteering to be an seducer by separating himself into two parts, one in turning away from the laws of creation and by persuade his brothers, male and female to lead the human-groups into debauchery in the sense of procreative relations. It's not necessary to provide details of the whole story, most people know by refers in the Bible.

Let's move to the present modern times, most of what has been spoken has been in refers to past events and situations, knowing the past is not something that is distinct or separated from the present, only each moment cause one to think of the moment as past or future, where in the moment past or present causes a reaction of an event or situation to manifest as a form of creation.

When in response to any call for clarity, one takes the time or opportunity to assure others ones greatest for accepts of what is being given.

In the information that have been given the full understanding of all the material may not set right to you now, but as time moves on it will open to you. We are going back to Consciousness. All events of the past eras we are trying to recover from the mishaps and deception, hatred, all types of worry doing. In so doing our conscious-mind need to stop accepting opinions of people without a clue about the nature of mind or the natural order of life.

Rather you understand or not, there are creative powers in the works for humanity that will bring in good results which will better mankind in the long-run.

The Divine destiny is the natural order for one to be evolved in ones individual consciousness to be blessed.

Let's move to another type of thought in question, "How can one respect life"?

First in order to respect something or someone, one must "know" what's really meant by the word "Respect," one believe in honor and or appreciate things and being obedient to the Higher order which demands that law to be respected.

Another thought, what is life and how do we or you respect it? Or do you respect it? Is life just a physical thing to you, a mask to act out your illusive fascinate of desire to work good or bad! Or is it just the unknown to you?

Let's envision some of the concepts that construe the thought about life. Another question, are humans living in an elusive world with its concerns that we know or are there a real meaning unknown to the average person yet to be discovered?

In saying again one must understand to be able to respect anything or view –point about life, if in the dark about any, just say it, "You Don't Know," it's no shame in not knowing but it's a shame when you don't seek out the understanding.

All the things one focus on in their everyday lives is just robotic for survive of the physical being, knowing the physical depends on that survival for the spiritual part to evolve. We sleep, we work, we eat, we become emotional in the feeling of sadness, happiness, pain and smile at times through it all etc. We live from day to day wondering why things are as they are in our lives, not understanding we are living in a "delusional world of activity.

We humans are destined to awake out of sleep that binds them in ignorance about what is real in life. As we come to the close of this cycle into the new age of Aquarian, we come more into the Light of Truth about ourselves and entities on this planet. Along with our judgment calls and planning will take a new turn for the better and we will stop developing events which will destroy all of us on this planet. In the past humans have permitted obstacles to program our minds in the way of destruction hatred, narrowness of understanding, obsession with material things, and the up-raise in unmoral activity, it's time to put down the foolish things that destroy life. And take up things for the real purpose for being and then we can respect life for its purpose.

Understanding with the heart brings the comprehension at the love-wisdom level which would allow ones soul to grasp the meaning of the past events, but realizing the true intended for broaden and assist to render for one to become more spiritual that which bring all-things into its reality. The heart-center wisdom quickens one's ability to grasp the truth which only is known by the wisdom of the heart-center.

Accordance to texts humans is to be the caretakers of other life-forms (species) on the planet. Let face it many humans are not equipped with the concern or no-how to care for themselves, so why think they would be concern or being conscious of the need for others.

First of all we need to stop thinking all humans are conscious, it's obvious that all are NOT, if they were they would realize every living things or life form give a gift to other life- forms all which carries the spark from the Source of life and it's capable of offering a specific gift to others forms or species, known there is no exceptions

There are species of life that have many gifts, some can help others to open-up spiritually and physical-improvements, others implant the concept that nature surround us, and one is willing to open one's mind to the reality of life they will see for themselves.

Ones soul can open to the energies from the higher realms and one can be lead to the reality of love in the heart-center that we all shared our-self individually in the truth from within our heart center, we are one in creation.

Let's think about the things most people have heard about in their life time along the theological terms or views, the Master of Masters Jesus the Christ, who was the embodiment of the Immaculate Concept, which was the Divine Design of the Source of all Life to follow. In the Christian biblical texts Jesus describes the law of cause and effect, by saying; "whatever you sow, you shall reap'! As a man think in his heart so is he" Do unto others what you would like others to do unto you. It's meaning what you do to self and what you do all creation in life, not just humankind, but all kingdoms in and on the earth which represent life relative speaking... If one has no knowledge of what life was meant to be in reality, how can one respect that which h/s cannot understand?

Another saying by Jesus, "the kingdom of heaven is at hand." What is really being said, or its meaning, well let's picture the Christ-Perfection being manifested in all of us which mean being focus on the laws placed in our hearts and minds to do what is required of us along the lines of growth in one first. We are to develop the Christ-Consciousness in its fullness or what we call Christ-Perfection, for our to have it working in our lives every day in the relative-form, if you are wondering why, because of that litter spark of the Divine within us to be able express it's ability.

One must start somewhere so let's begin with what it takes to walk on the path of reality in truth, it's time to retrain ones mind and become balance knowing it's the key to a better place within oneself where happiness of one's soul comes in play. Balance is a keynote, it is so important, there are so many challenges and lessons to awaken us to the inner parts of mankind to be explored it is unlimited. To be balance one must take all areas possible in the sense of relativity.

Let speak about one area many overlook the "inner senses," those which allow one to pick-up information, thoughts, and mental images of Highest Planes that were always intended to be strongly tied to the physical senses, as they were thousands of years ago when humankind was more in touch with the Higher Realities. As humankind gravitated towards materiality (things) and focus became unbalance their attention was of physical matters, not on the things what really matters.

The major quality which is lacked in humanity is balance in living, one's life in the middle-way or we can say as above, so below which brings a form of balance between the higher you (self) and the lower you (self). All of this brings understanding to the middle –way between the heavens and earth.

As humans come into the Light of truth they will receive true freedom, the original course of life will demand everyone to master their lower-self and expand into the true Light of the Source the (Absolute) God, to receive the out pouring of the completeness of the relative evolvement of the earthly kingdoms.

We are to abide within our higher mental state to become acquainted with the vibrations of one's spiritual self. Although it's, not meant to make one become, tense because this is a somewhat unpleasant vibration to some sincere sweet persons. Do the best you can and guardians of our growth and the Source of life will do the rest?

There is another area needs to be fully addressed and that's ones free-choice or will we humans use it so freely as something to say or do, but in reality it is so misunderstood, more think its means to be free to do whatever one wants, whenever the desire speaks to one conscious mind to do so.

The original purpose of this gift, of free-choice was to attain ones sense-consciousness to the Divine Ideal of Love, not for the individual whims and appetites, but

Attain their sincere effort to express the Divine qualities in the ordinary person. We humans pride ourselves in being the Image of God as you say, but do you really know about that image; it's not just what some believe, it's using The Divine Qualities that are permitted to us to have use of.

There is a story about someone who used those divine qualities, in Exodus 14:21 of Old Testament- Christian translation, it says, Moses as he stretched out his hand over the sea; and the lord caused the sea to go back by the strong wind and the sea divided. So you see an average man using the divine qualities given to him can work, now look at that very special person who was fully developed with his divine and human parts of one's body Jesus in the New Testament, in Matthew 8: 26 spoke to his disciples "Why are you fearful. O you of little faith? Then he arose and rebuked the winds and the sea, and there was a great calm. In saying these two examples when the emotional activity coupled with ones thoughts can create things for good or wrong by ones will to make it so. The same power that is in both Moses and Jesus is in you and me, by us not asset or accepting it, we are ignoring its existence.

If only individuals would make the sincere effort in discipline of their human sense-consciousness until they learn total obedience to the image of God pattern of perfection.

The purpose of the activity of life is love for Life, not only human life, but all life. If the beings of divinity knowingly and respectfully act on the law of god in not intrude upon our rights of free-will or choice, of individuals, as they know it is the human-birthright, so why do many think we are any different in our requirements to live?

Think about this, we pride ourselves in being an image of God-Father, but are we becoming what are required to be that image, believe it or not everything comes with a price even your divine self to manifest to its fullness of accelerated being.

Yes it was the original idea in the beginning the image and likeness of the Source (God) was to manifest in each of us, but individual do change purpose by their desires to carry forward good or backward evil thoughts and activities.

If, ones will is to learn about life, one must dip deep into the relative thoughts and feeling of the sources of our purpose in life, which will lead to one becoming the expression of the superhuman (God-person) that conditions us in the qualities and transgender of the ideals of masters of Love, light and wisdom. Only through these forces can humanity understand how to attain to the Divine image of love, which enchants all life

Let us spring up from the ashes of ignorance and live in a world of peace with all life, and with respect for it. Listen with your inner being to receive the true- self.

Awaken to the light of truth within you, where you can receive the Christ-Consciousness it will become commonplace and functional in ones Divine part.

Most of you are not yet ready to enter into a closer relationship with the Divine inner- part of yourselves it takes voluntary and cooperative effort, to be really true to yourself, are you willing?

Human- beings have a tendency to become imprisoned in the old concepts of being less or inferior to other forms of life outside the earth realm. These are misleading concepts, stop and focus on the areas which are important right now, one must seek knowledge of life right here and now on earth, get right with the kingdoms of earth first, that means respect all-life on earth first in all its forms here now.

No one can be truly happy, without you having love and respect for life, in ones hearts and minds this can only be received through the knowledge from within.

The thought of you being something special, is enough to bring a form of peace and happiness, the mystery it all should place a light bulb on within to light up your minds.

We cannot be happy with just a half of anything, our true nature requires us to be completed in our purpose, and what is that purpose do we really know? Life can be so unmoving in any direction at a given time, Some of us are amazed and others are unmoved by many of the phenomenon or events that opens the heart, and mind, but many have grown cold, for many just play its last song without thought of the How or Why, which opens the heart to love.

The last tone is independent of the cycle waiting for the moment of insensitivity to change that never ending ultimate ignorance, which hold mankind captive drawing destroying attention to its life-forces.

In some cases although not all of humanity has previously been following a conventional series of lives might suddenly become inspired to change their life and strive to climb out of the common mold and gain a deeper understanding of the impotence of learning and open to what it means to know the reason of one's existence.

So, an individual is born into a life-pattern and when receive content with others, watch their patterns, make changes and others don't change for the better.

We humans are the representation which plays upon the senses or the field of consciousness can borrow its space only from the past events of what one calls a succession which has been cinematized in time.

With the Aquarian Age or New Age fully coming in, an age where the ideals are based on Liberty, Equality, and most of all, freedom to love oneself and ones Creative Source The presence of this new cycle of Aquarian moving into its full manifestation and the expanding perfection of humankind consciousness the glorious cord of electronic life energy is connecting each one of us with the God presence to enforce the new Age of love (universal) into manifestation which join the earth kingdoms with the "One main Source of life existence in this Universal Galaxy, which completes the connection of the earth to the first heaven. "As Above, So Below," that glorious Bridge from humankind to the Divine, meaning the bridge bring the world (earth) into its true Light and all there on to connect with the god's world and restore its oneness with life as we all know to be life. Hopefully this will be the final victory for earth and its inhabitants to overcome.

In this new privilege union we humans will dress ourselves in the garments of the light of god's Love no-longer have the need for seeking the Light it will illuminate our entire being with the everlasting Light.

Many of this world's population have forgiven the real beginning of the components of life. There are ten components; the ten components services life, the elements which substances life, are Air, Water, Fire, and Earth. Just think about it, without these things no life on the plant can live. Air is the second primary element of creation; A condition of gases, and intelligence of thousands of frequency levels, thee essence of all manifestations which substances all life without boundaries. The second component Water is the third basic element, in recent years water was discovered on at least three other plants in our Solar System, including possibly on our Moon in the form of ice. It's the element primary forms which liquid can exist; refers to origin of everything. The third component, but the first primary element Fire, without fire or heat no life forms on earth will be able to survive. As for the Earth it's a vibration frequency forming in solid quality. It's the fourth globe in the planetary chain. The primary element is to function to substance the needs of the life-forms, which inhabitant s its planes. All of these Elements makes up of this universal needs, evolved in the fist round of the planet, also known as the clear Light of the beginning a condition necessary for the primary element electricity to exist.

The purpose is not only the general needs, but for the cycle patterns of the evolutional changes and growth of earth and all there on animated and inanimate things that are of the earth, it's a living entity.

I would like to express my own feelings about a part of life that many people do not think about the "Sacred Game," know thy-self. Some time I catch myself being overwhelm in thoughts of reviewing my mistakes and wondering if I had did things differently how would things turn out and it would have been better for me?

I also have found myself fantasize the future. Now I stop and am in the moment I would see the beauty in the now.

We humans waste a good part of our time in life dwelling on regrets and fantasy. Not saying one should not review past or hope for the future to be better than the now. What, I am saying not let it cloud the moment slip by without being great-full for the moment it's good for a lot of reasons unknown to us. The things we take for gratuity like our breath, our heart beat, the movement of the blood in our veils the air that touch our bodies, the sun which gives heat, there are so many things in the moment we overlook.

I find myself busy at times thinking of the situations for the moment which is overwhelming at the time, so seen times I forget the good things for that moment. After the moment I realize How Blessed I am to be privilege to be thought of by the Source of life to be bring forth into existence.

I am, one who at times needs to council me, we all have our times of weakness, I know there it much to learn, it make me have headaches at times to formulae the thoughts which comes in my mind.

Nowadays with all the deception of others we need help to broke free at times. I catch myself more and more trying to see the beauty in all life, but some people make it hard at times, knowing I have an option to worry about things going wrong around me and to me at times or just trust the Source of life to fix-it and realize my Divine Source it the only One who can fix-it right.

The truth is that each of us is a work in progress as we focus our minds on the spiritual aspects of our nature we are touched by our inner guide knowing everything it made right for that moment. It keeps us looking forward to the stillness that keeps us in the present moment of peace. Yes we know, we are living in an age where the lessons come faster and faster and situation are stronger pulling one's heart sting crying for release and one's soul is push into new growth. As we grow we began to listen to more the inner voice that will sent guidance, but also one will hear messages of profound enlightenment and beauty.

As we move into the new cycle of earth and humankind in their evolutional stage therefore, it's imperative one to be conscious of the reality of whom and what we are.

If one strives for truth and freedom knowing the only way to receive true freedom is to know truth its factor which gives both. During the preparation for this truth to manifest clarity comes by one's own desire and conscious command to be open to truth.

We can only have clarity when the One Eternal Truth and Freedom by awaking one own consciousness to the law of life which detects Love, Harmony, Peace and unity with all Life-forms on planet earth.

"And Os Be It"

RESPECT FOR LIFE

This is the final chapter of this book and it may seem a subject matter at first untouchable to some, but I believe it's a must to be addressed.

All relationships in existence are very important in ever perspective, we look through our nature eyes, what we see all masses of forms and these forms are seen as different substance. The appearances are a distinction of each thing.

For example; in order for there to be you and I these has to be consensual boundaries that create an appearance of a distinction between you and I, like the different between a chair and a table, the spare, but the same material as a tree.

These conceal boundaries constitutes how we normally perceive the world, how we live at the explicate level of form.

The universe has given a great gift to life as we know it holds all learning and challenges. Each life entity holds promise and yet easy is vulnerable to the difficulties and challenges, which, influences the vary existence in ones environment, our lives depend on other life forms for our survival, the food we eat, the animals and the vegetation, for the mush part we don't say, "Thank you", for their part in our survival, don't you understand they to must be shown respect too. Their lives are importance they have souls too.

There is only one-way humankind can have true freedom and be released from the wheel of birth and rebirth is when one individually starts acting on that One Law of Love, which brings harmony and peace with the understanding of ALL LIFE IS ONE, we all must respect it.

The development of the knowledge of the "I" is given to humans and not the other kingdoms as it's been said, many believe other forms of life have a collective conscious. The so-call lower expressions of life at present, although they are conscious of their outer world; their own desires, craving and feelings because their consciousness reflect upon their thoughts and acts. Also we have some human- forms, which show the lower development and that show him/her it not aware of the "I" consciousness and the importance of life.

Respect for life is very important by reason all living things share the same functions to live, for example; all life have apparatus which function in a some-what different ways, and some like human, take the Brian as it's control center in the physical sense as for all animal life, humans alike, now the other forms like vegetation (plant-life) or an trees, the control- center is invisible to the human eye. As for those ones who disregard any life form; need to first think hard about our physical bodies in their sense organism.

Let's speak on some of these functions, we all share being apart of what we call-life; the animal kingdom, humans include all have the stimulation of senses which causing them to function correctly for their given purpose.

Let's speak of these senses, sight-its one of the elementary senses, but the most evolved sense, because it register the intensity of the light waves and color vibrations of the light-waves coming contact with the complexities of the organ desired for sight. There others senses that we must realize all life functions the same way as part of life we share in common, the sense of touch and feelings, although it's regarded as one of the elementary senses, which others have evolved. The sense of touch and feelings operates by means of certain nerves which are on the outer covering of the skin and also in the internal organism of the body. We also become aware of changes or conditions in our bodies such as hunger, thirst, other internal sensations such as pain and pleasures. The sense of hearing is a delicate nerve in the inner part of the ear. The Car drum or the tympanum vibrates in response to the air-vibration or sound-waves reaching it from the outside surroundings, these impressions and pass it on to the sub-conscious part of the Brian.

These vibrations are intensified, and auditory nerve-ends take up the impresses by the sound-waves according to pitch, which causes the life form to precept one of fear, love, danger etc. In addressing the importance to understand the need to respect life for it maybe the only thing one can say we all share.

Humanity must move forward and upward in consciousness to greater and greater development to one's spiritual clarity. Where, ones conscious is there the individual is functioning. When one becomes spiritual knowing Divine Love will never cease to exist.

By this being the last chapter the closing of refection of the evil mankind do in their ignorance, seem to define their present state of being.

Mankind over- look, the simple small things that have an effort on ones activity and belief about life and the people around them.

For whatever reasons the average person deeds are confine to immoral or moral, there are good deeds many are doing, but the information is not put out there for people to see or hear about. Unfortunate for many the media, newspapers, television, and advertisement form on topics that influence the minds of the people unawareness of the methods which are being use to under-mind them in getting them to buy things they really do not want, also to place fear and sorrow in the people. The advertisements get you to feel you need this or that or you are sick and need this type of medicines. The media pull the evil thoughts of mankind and their evil deeds on the general pupil. There are good people in the world and there are just as many good deeds that are being done as evil one, you would not know it by the forms of communication that we receive from the reports. They place and suggest things that inter the mind that you personally need their product or pills because you are ill or think you are, by saying ask your doctor, and that's, if the doctor says it's okay it must be, not so. Think FOR YOURSELF, no one has all the answers.

You may think what can we do stop the harmful suggestions that impinge upon ones consciousness? Stop listening to the news, stop reading the new- paper, and periodical some books that would have you believe that life is full of only evil doers, stop being trapped in it, with no rescores, look at special reports which warring about dangers situations.

We take life cycles for granted or one can say the operation which applies to everything and to being in the universe relativity speaking, the operation or regulation of the natural events. We also over look the beauty of life with its laws which governs our lives, the flux and reflux of operation of everything.

Cycles in life are so common place that we overlook them in operation, think about it, the air ones breath, the light we see by and darkness, the weather changes the water we drink, and the earth under one's feet we walk on, all the small changes. One cannot imagine what the world would be like if the repetition of light and darkness. The nature of change is the cyclic progress for evolvements our development is dependent upon the changes in character-building, and soul reviewing.

Cycles in the natural order of things is like a wheel turning forward or backward all in the chose we make for our life. In learning the reason of the cycles it will become self opening to how and why in time as one grows to be a self-conscious individual. Life is a mystery on the most part, because many people don't ask of one self, and seeking answers from the Source of life for the reasons why or how.

In life the question may take some time to revival itself, knowing only what one see with ones neutral eyes is not enough for clear understanding, life is a mystery and expresses itself in different ways, so it becomes beyond ones comprehension.

I wrote a book call "Open to the Magic Within," in 2005, where I talked about a bridge that needed mending, the idea came from a dream, I kept dreaming over and over for a span of two years, somewhat different each time, the bridge so I wrote what I thought was the meaning at the time, I know it was a message for me in some way. I am a little wiser now. The first part brought me to the understanding we all have a bridge to be mended. But it's so much to the meaning, so I will give my readers the rest, of my bridge story-meaning it was not only for me to cross the broken bridge but mend it too. I will be as brief as possible, there are two areas to consider, one being the lower- selves, and the higher self, which brings a dividing line between the two and that is the bridge of illusion between the two dimensions the bridge is this link, just as Divine and mankind.

A navigational system is used to mend that bridge between the lower-self and the higher-self to the Divine-self. The understanding came to me! I understood that as I grow in wisdom to the meaning of life and what is required of me to mend my own bridge, I would be able to assist others in their quest for wholeness too. As I expanded in consciousness more clarity came to me, its reality that has to come forth in my mind, that in order to mend my bridge, I be willing to let go of the illusions and unwanted the old experiences in my past to be no longer in control by my lower-self, moving subconscious trash and letting my higher-self take completely in control knowing in time I will have mended my bridge and the Divine –perfected-self will assist my ascension into the Light beyond what humankind thinking as being holy, but the sight of being in oneness with all life in the cosmic universal all of holy-ones.

While I was working on this book I was going though many life challenges which question my thought in doing good will pay, don't let anyone tell you they are not looking for a reward for doing good, they are fooling them –selves, everyone is looking for something back, even if only a smile or say, thank you, I am being honest with you I never thought I would ever be in some situations, I have experience because I am a good person at-heart, but knowing as I do, life cycles changes, situations change, people change, and conditions change. I know within my heart that things will change for my betterment, all is for my learning, and I will not fall or fail in my quest for a better life or be a better person, while I am here I will still seek higher levels in my spirituality and natural learning in my life quest, seeking the physical manifestation of all my goals. The best part of life is my development and journey which brings purpose inward into the unknown of my spiritual requirements until the final change.

There are times in each of our lives cycle changes brings with it challenges to make us grow closer to our Source and after it's over one feel better about the challenge. With me many changes from one thing to another and the situation seem to be getting out-of hand at times, I admit at times I felt a feeling of disillusionment and wondered if it's worth it, to try to be a better person, knowing others are moving right along doing evilness to others seem to get-by in their acts and things seems to go right for them. But then I begin to think, what am I thinking, those are the ones not growing, in their true purpose, I am Blessed, because every time a challenge come I learn something new, so I try to overcome the feeling that I was slow in my growth.

This is what I call "self-Counsel," although I've been given a hard time by others, who have use deceptive activities in some of the situations. I am great-full to be beyond the illusions so many are in at this time. I ask my Divine Source to open or illuminate my mind to things of the (truth) and as I listen, a soft inner voice within me began to speak, "I will give you the answers to the mysteries of life, if you stand the test." (Challenges) that come, and there is no weapon that is formed against you will proclaim victory over you." "I AM the Light and Truth, and you will overcome all wrong doers and their deeds against you."

So my bridge is being mended by my growth on the spiritual path. Knowing that the only way to make ones ascension into the Light of Truth and Love stand in ones belief of that which is "Greater."

One needs to focus on issues, but not overly concern, it's important to release your focus on unworthy issues, like wars and other vices which destroy the forms of life. Be concern with that which effects life, the good parts, nature and the other inhabitants. Follow the Spiritual Warrior Path and ask for protection as you travel the road of life.

The requirements for the survival of earth and the inhabitants is the growth may totally disrupt what many have intended and the desire outcome may elude them and yet what many regard as disruption, and blockages of desires and failures and death is just an opportunity for union and reverse of what been wrong with the activities though the ages.

The last words, associate with those who love life and have a respect for life of all life forms, a devotion and concern are to be enforced on life. Your responsibility and response as individuals is to take action on a level which is higher then you have ever done before speak out to those who make the laws for protection of the natural environment and the other creatures living in union with us on earth working its purpose.

The path of conduct is an important issues, one must have courage and dedication to achieve the goal of survival of earth and its inhabitants.

We all need to become conscious of our essences and bring into form the expression of love and unity of life by respecting all life. A great power has made and it making life force available to you and all life forms to expend all energy now. Let the whispering voice which Speak to your heart "Respect Life."

After all that's been said and done in this book in reflection on the activities of humanity in the past and present it's to stop and just "Think," to oneself, in all my experiences do I really see or can I discover change or do I realize a change must come?

In life each of us from time to time needs to have our inner viewpoint of life refreshed, have it directed to a new and higher level.

Life should provide inspiration which helps us to gain the "Greatest Good," from life in itself, by realizing life is good if we live according to the laws of life. One must journey through life evolving the soul, and spirit in oneself, these are the facets for progress to ones Greatest Good.

All humans are in constant change, hopefully evolving and willing to withdraw the vibrating on the lower planes of existence. The spirit, within wants to break through the barrier of ignorance and direct the soul of each individual to a better way of living by a respect for all life. Once this barrier is overcome the activities of savagery and hatred, will be over the individual will begin to climb upward toward ones freedom from darkness into the Light of reality of the true destiny of all humanity.

In order to recover humanity is to awake and become the controller of one's individual life by doing what is right, Stop being lead by the moment emotional feeling that brings on destruction of life in any form.

All activities of wrong doing has engulf the planet, by those who create pain and suffering to the different forms of life, be mindful wrong-doer will pay the full penalty for their activity and the truth of those destructive activities will be known and the veil of deceptive and all evil also will be shown to all who are willing to see truth.

The clouds that hide the Light in these days and time will be consumed and mankind will no longer suffer the pain of needs for peace and harmony. But before true peace and harmony can come one must ask for forgiveness of their own individual wrong-deeds and then forgiveness for others wrong doings as well. For there are none who will escape their own creations, how can you think or not be willing to put aside the important of this statement.

I hold the highest vision of God desire for humankind to come forth now to fulfill the true purpose of our being. The spirit within each of us is required to come forth and be the image of our Maker. I envision peace, unity and love between all people when the veil is remove from their eyes. When all people become Spiritual Beings and become completely oppose and repel all evil intend from those who live a life of evil and hearts and mind are blind.

Ask yourself be honest because you are the only one who can answer what is honesty in regard to oneself. Question, are you oppose to facing what reality is or are you still willing to accept only half-true or the illusive world? Are you aware that Archaeology has found discoveries that would change the history books, but because of the confusion they would causes they permit continues believe untruth.

Down through time mankind lived and practice falsehood of the purpose of life and about life, so it's hard to change in mid-stream of your life, but dear ones it's time to take control of your own lives in the spirit of truth and love. Remove those old blinder and old patterns make-way for the new life, now it's time to receive the true immaculate-conception within your hearts and minds, the yoke of false hood will change into what's certain in reality.

Have a desire to conscious- connect and link ones human-mind with the cosmic-mind, which we call God, as one contact the higher mind of the self an open door to the reality of oneself which will come respect for all life and the shame turn to honor of life, knowing the true reality of life is Love, peace, and respect for all life.

In all the examples and events we have talked about, this does not cause you to think about it, there is a barrier in one's heart. These things is not for judgmental responds, but only for enlighten to the facts which face us as human-being with a heart and love for life.

The inward powers of the mind are potentially illimitable, but they lie dormant and unexpressed as you can see by the events and conditions of the earth and it's inhabited at present.

Humanity as a whole need to stop being a collective-mind set for wrong activities, each one an individual –mind set to chose the path which brings clarity to the individual.

As of now in this moment it's in the past, time for a new beginning. As, you have listened to the distracting voices of the imperfect unsatisfying life of the senses. You have been pulled this way and that way, by desire, by impulses, by uncontrolled emotions, and have been influenced by the advice of those who have no clue or have no inward knowledge.

First, change the consciousness to go forth into a self-mastery and turning to the light of love and truth to awaken of one's true-self in how we are to act and feeling toward all on the planet.

We all can receive this good; I cannot impress too strongly upon you my dear ones, how necessary it is to be open to change in one's mind about life and all the purposes for all life-forms.

Let the feeling of love for life pull at your heart-sting for the fullness of the true-love in the expanding until it envelops and saturate your entire being with the love for all life.

We are to emulate the God within us as a gift to benefit all life. I implore you do not delay in showing love to all life. One thing we must be conscious of that's which ever form on the planet plant, animal, human, whatever form of life share a common Source of existence that manifest in different body types, but all is One and the Same brought us to earth in a specific form with a Divine power to awaken for the purpose that is to service "Life."

Dear ones the planet is in trouble from the human destructive devices use against life on the planet. Be it known these are not just idle words. It's time to stop where you are and face the truth about life and respect it. Not just from ones lips, but from within one's heart.

One must say these words, "Within myself, I will overcome the madness; I will turn a deaf-ear to all these voices and listen only to the voices within my higher-spirit, which always speaks with the wisdom of pure perfect universal-mind of the Source of all life." No more shall I be perplexed and worried about what tomorrow bring, but to be guided on my path in life by the true Source of life, focusing my mind on the highest Good and being respectful of all life.

"Humanity awake for your time is far shorter than you know. "And So It Will Be"

I hold the flame of peace and Love for life within my heart to pervade the world
> *I See the Light within All I see as it flows*
> *Filling the World with All its wonders*
> *Command all to take its Rightful Place in the Cosmos*
> *As it absorbs the Light of Love from the true Source of Life- God*

I send out these thoughts to all humanity from within the core of my being with only love that can measure what one can show in relative terms of understanding by the human spirit. I love all life it matters not what form of life because Life is God's Love.

My heart and spirit has been enchanted by the love within me for all life, and the love and beauty veiled in the different forms of life and their colors. My eyes gaze upon the beauty of life, with a warm feeling of understanding, what true love is. And only the inadequate (ignorant) ones can only hope to find, if they release, themselves from their cold hearts and from hatred and greed not knowing the reality of life, and things, in which they do not care to understand.

Stop and take a look around at the beauty of the earth and the many inhabitants and really all life form on earth are the inheritance of this plant and do has an effect on the other, makes no diffident which form of life we all feel the effects.

There are changes taking place, the processes of change even in lighten in the sky and how is has changed and you notice the seasons and its weather.

The sum total of what has accused in the form of world events good or evil is living history, but the events are forth coming are shadows cast as results of the past. There will come a time when the seeming impossible of the deeper truth of our purpose in living in harmony with all life will come. When that moment comes the rational intellect will comprehend, what seem to be impossibility. It's when humanity comes out of sleep from its embryonic state to reach to a place to expand their divinity and essence to mirror.

In relative speaking terms, because of the three dimensional view and the general opinion of said learned Pythagoreans stated "the universe and all that is in it is determined by the number three, since beginning and middle and end give the number three of the universe."

Let us take this thought as our starting point, all natural bodies and magnitudes are capable of motion through nature it is either a straight line or circular or a combination, I know you are wondering how we came to this point, of lines and circles?

It's about the principle of movement that is in place, all locomotion as we term it is either straight or circular.

Let's think about the circle as being the symbol of completion, but in motion it only moves around and around in one place. Not changing the subject but think about humanity continuance going around and around for thousands of years with hatred in their hearts for others in war's to no end, where is the love? Where is the evolvement of mankind in conscious of the need for peace?

Now that I have told you thing that mankind has created through not understanding a change is in order for life on this plant to get better for all of life forms, not just humans, and the human need to stop believing they are the only ones and come to the reality that they are Not in control.

It's time now to change for the better as we precept life to be, we are on the threshold of a new beginning.

The Aquarian Age is a new chance for humanity to evolve and enter the spiritual age, can you see the signs, and it is a new age now, an age where mankind can receive a higher cosmic influence, which can cleanse the entire earth of past non-constructive activity. Civilization in-part will go through tremendous changes in morals, and values, social structure between all colors of people will change, will be as one people, I say colors because there is only one race the human-race.

It's time to awaken be one with the Source of creation in your consciousness the self knowing that you are sustain by and through that substance which makes you One with the God of your being.

I wonder if some of you ever stop and thought about your real origin (starting point), if you become conscious of the true awakening, the knowledge will open to you through the Great all-seeing eye of one's inner-self (soul). Knowing trying to state innocence of wrong doing or the lack of cunning will not help in the long-run, we can only be free if by seeking knowledge of the truth of who we are in realty.

Question, do you really believe that we came from dust of the ground or from a fish in the sea through evolution? Another question, do you think these are just signs and symbolisms systems as to comprehend the un-comprehensive?

Do you want to know what I think about? To me life is truly a mystery and I believe one unfolds in their potential attributes of perfection into wholeness and upward movement of one's consciousness to the original state of being as one with the Source of Life.

Just think about it, in reality we all are gods in creation and gods in manifestation of all the things we say and do, even when we don't understand the mechanics of what we do... It is time for the appearances of life to take a backset and move into the reality of life and act like we really are gods by design.

Understand, we all are One in creation not just we humans, but all living forms of life there is no lesser in the working of creation.

The working of progression is in all life it grows from the slower vibrations frequencies to faster vibration frequencies; progression from one state of consciousness to a higher state of consciousness, the progressive growth and perfection is in all is manifest in the universes.

Learn to enter the center of your being, that real place of truth to enlighten you and as you do the next step will be seen opening of the new consciousness about how your thought about all life will change for the better and by learning one will enter into the Great Cosmic stratum which is the realm of evolutional consciousness, when you become one in thoughts and feeling about the purpose of life it to become one, we all can work toward a better world order of love and peace toward all life on earth and rid humanity of its shame once and for all.

There is a question do you want to hear this? Some may think by becoming a good person it may take all the fun out of life or some may think good people must give of their freedom to be bad or good. Some may say I don't want to change, I like who I am now. Other may not see a need for change. Question, are you true to yourselves about changes? It is something you really don't want? Or is it something you feel you will miss (your save-zone)?

There are some feel that it's moving toward all-things being balance and they do not want to feel or overcome by others, these are the ones who desire to be in control, in reality no one is really in total control.

The average person do not think or concern about life in all its mysteries, it takes seeking to receive, understanding what the law of life requires of us, the only thing we can do is to seek change in the best way for the betterment of all life, know change is coming and those who refuse to change will be left behind in the darkness of the true reality of life, know it's a gift to all of us. As the present time it's only a spark, we need to stop circling in the old world of the past.

On the other hand the circle can be looked at as being never ending brilliance and radiance, as never ending connection of possibilities of richness in the world as an eternal blaze, but understand this can only come with change..

Now if one takes the straight line, although it's been said that the straight line is contrary because it moves in directions up or down, forward or backward, and the circular motion is oppose to the straight line action. The circle is complete in its stagnation movement. The straight line on the other hand one can make a choice to go forward, backward, up or down all of which leads to achievement for productivity or unconstructive activity by the chosen path on that straight line in direction. The circle only goes around and around without achievement it's gold is naught direction, as we look at the circle and the straight line both are open to change in synchronizing mind and body, trusting self to express growth, whither being in a circle or straight line mood.

Every discoverer of the treasures of life, and its purpose will receive the insight to what is beyond the human expression at present will elevate to the majestic rhythm of the universal life.

The Human Embryo feels at peace and silence when their eyes are close as it

Listen to the spirit within its heart, saying "I offer my love to the heavenly Father and to heavenly Mother," and to the Divine Teachers to feed my spirit." The Embryo is the beginning of a new birth in formed in the astral world with its casing of new thought energy still around it, as it grows from within the mother's body living on earth.

The earth is like the study of human history before mankind became conscious of what and who they were. Think about the different in the earth as it illustrates its principle make-up and the changes with its narrow parallel Mountain ridges, there rise about the same time the level, caused a remarkably even sky line as it was viewed from one summits, the sky line marks approximately the surface of what was a plain early on in the Cenozoic era. River, develop and carved out valleys and kept their course they formed large streams parallel to the valleys stand out coast lines and the great events of sea water.

In this new era, we will be salvaging a new body out of the old, but a new consciousness of humanity where humankind will have evolved to understand that it must be as above, so it must be below. The two triangles represent the root-substance of all life between the interplay of creation relative to life on earth, the shadowy end, the matter-end.

Having these things clearly in mind, we can really come to the place of the ultimate spring of one's spirit, which is founded upon the framework of being, the principles or aspects or qualities of humankind. It's been said that mankind is mainly developed from three different hierarchies, or states, from three different planes of being. The lowest comes from the earth, the middle, and the intellectual-intuitional, thirdly the supreme seed of the universe or universal cosmos.

The more important thing in this book is the subject RESPECT FOR LIFE OF ALL FORMS.

Respect for life would not be complete without a smile for the elements with brings forth life of all kinds. As we behold all the forms of life stand to celebrate its own form of life, the Lord said "Behold my forms by the hundreds and the thousands manifold and Divine, various in shapes and hue." Behold all the god's and Angles; Behold many wonders that no one has ever seen before.

There is a Love which brings smiles and weeping, has no bound nor end, where the Love of life meet where the rising of the Sun and as the night hide in silence of darkness.

Beloved ones open your hearts and minds to the thoughts of love (Divine) and feel your divinity and your ability to express that love to all life with which you have contact everyday upon your individual path. The greatest expression of God's love is the changing of you to make the world a better place!

Beloved ones open your hearts and minds to the Love of God and ask that the full measure of His Divine Love be poured into the cup of your individual consciousness as you experience this blessing, and let the quality of Divine Love flow into all ideas and inspirations. Love is not merely an emotional feeling you experience for others and life in general, it also must include the understanding of how to express that feeling of God' faithfulness to you in the idea of creativeness of you in your beginners, its Divine Love which can work for you to bring forth the perfectness into manifestation you so deeply desire.

This close's of the subject of respect for all life, we as individuals could come to the realization of life, something we can not over look or close our eyes too. We humans are only one part of life, this world in all its inhabitants are many forms of life.

We are "One" in creation from the same Source of life, and we all are function for our own purpose in that form of life. Understand although different forms nothing is separate all functions are in unison the elements, the plants, the animals, only mankind seem to have problems in becoming unified. Are we so blind that we don't question our own reasons for the purpose of life, can! Can we control the flow of thought's which controls the mind, that part which brings truth?

"Beloved Presence of God within each of us
I love and adore you, I give thank to your comforting
Presence of Divine Love
"AND SO IT IS, IT DONE"

CLOSING REMARKS

As Tears Flow with hopes for Smiles

Something I wrote in two thousand and five, (2005) a poem that sprang up in my heart.

The stream of yesterday's goodbyes, the joy and pain, perhaps the wasted time could have been productive! Wounded by ones own misunderstanding seeing ones dreams crushed as an apple with ones teeth.

Misfortune of so many in memories weeping seeing the pain of others tears to wipe's away the pain. As tear turns into a smile when new dreams are born and true love is shown as many gather and move aside the walls of hatred and disappointment, which separates the hearts. All the Tears will be wiped away, and the smiles will return as first thought.

We become like puppets as the infinite and our cup direct us are filled with tears and smiles, as the mysteries unmask themselves to our humilities soothes our spirit. As we love humankind and unite our spirits with one thought and that is to love one another unconditionally.

Only our spirits can understand the beauty of a tear and a smile as they reflect from the mirrors of our livers, describing the inner being. We are unable to hid ones nakedness.

The universe is ours to enjoy, the more we grow in love and virtues the more we stop the tears of sorrows and partake the freedom of being able to feel the joy that will bring the smiles.

Peace and Love

LAST THOUGHTS OF THE TREASURIES OF THE HEART

On my last thoughts on the subjects in this book in it's ending, is a massage, to you're" is to love yourself more then anything outside of the Source that gives you life, all others loves are placed in their place like love-ones, family, friends, and others in the humankind, don't forget the animal-kingdom and the plants and trees, sea-life elements that feed us with their love.

In opening your heart to yourself, by speak sweet things to your heart and meaning the words it will bring you to the place of unconditional love for one-self

As you learn to love self and want to know the real you, then the truth about yourself will be open to you and you will see yourself for who you really are.

Once you know the truth about you, then you would be able to love all of life formers on the planet.

If you feel insecure, just put your hand over your heart and feel the vibrations and say "I love me, I accept me for what I am will commit myself to this real love I feel! I am important! I will make my life count for my good." Say this to yourself until you can feel its truth. Keep sending love to every part of you, your thoughts, emotional feeling, your desires of good and you will receive only the best within your heart and mind. And it will manifest on the outside.

In my conclusion, hopefully you who read my book will take what I've said to heart and help make changes in society to better all life on the planet. To Become an individual who will enrich life on the planet, as you engage your energies in activities to educate others, and one who process through life with purpose developing spiritual dexterity in understand of the laws of life.

There are so many who processed through life with no apparent purpose, just to feed ones appetites of the physical. One must unify to secure the entrance of the illumined spiritual consciousness first before our true blessing will manifest, in the ability to really understand your real purpose and who you really are and your true purpose...

And So It Is

THE COVER

I design this cover to show that I respect all parts of life as I believe life to be in its relativity of life on earth. This cover shows the unification of life as it should be.

The Source of life has and is still beautifying the earth with its creations, and its time that we humankind learn bring our minds out of bondage, with ignorance and see the true manifestation of all beauty is all forms of life.

As you sufficiently unfold to the understanding of the oneness of life and realize your identity, with all life forms all will become clear. This illustration is asking you to look beyond the picture and see the real meaning by looking around at life unfolding all around you in its beauty, from the lowest to the highest.

One must develop (feeling) a kinship to all forms, when you grasp this thought and concise your consciousness will open and you find yourself at-one-nests with all life on earth.

In time you will expand your consciousness out into the Universe to a greater region of ones mind advancement.

The part which shows the destinies are different forks use different ones for their guides, in working toward the true Source of life and to grasp the realization of life and the mastery of ones self, which bring the reality of truth to unfold in ones consciousness that you are the reality in this world of appearances.

As for the earth it's our presence home until we reach the ascended state, of no return.

The embryonic is a new beginner for humankind on earth. The embryo is applied to a multi-cellular cell or organism in its early stages of development and growth.

Life forms, animals and plants go through an embryonic stage. Where, as humans reach the level of perfection and purity, we become a new creation in the form of an embryo of clarity and divinity.

It's our purpose to impress upon all who read this book the importance of this information, to show you that the presence of truth is facing you I have taken all of you into my heart in love, to assist you in freeing "yourselves." By understanding WHO you really are a part of the whole Universal in the making by the Divine Plan. Understand there is nothing which has Life is omitted from the plan. We all must open our minds and heart to truth in all its forms to become free within ourselves

"Peace to all Life"